Rumi

100
SELECTED
POEMS

DELHI OPEN BOOKS

JALĀL AL-DĪN MUAMMAD RŪMĪ also known as Jalāl al-Dīn Mu ammad Balkhī Mevlânâ/Mawlānā but more popularly known simply as Rumi (30 September 1207 – 17 December 1273), was a 13th-century Persian poet, Hanafi faqih, Islamic scholar, Maturidi theologian, and Sufi mystic originally from Greater Khorasan in Greater Iran. Rumi's influence transcends national borders and ethnic divisions: Iranians, Tajiks, Turks, Greeks, Pashtuns, other Central Asian Muslims, and the Muslims of the Indian subcontinent have greatly appreciated his spiritual legacy for the past seven centuries. His poems have been widely translated into many of the world's languages and transposed into various formats. Rumi has been described as the "most popular poet" and the "best selling poet" in the United States.

Contents

A Moment Of Happiness

A moment of happiness,
you and I sitting on the verandah,
apparently two, but one in soul, you and I.
We feel the flowing water of life here,
you and I, with the garden's beauty
and the birds singing.
The stars will be watching us,
and we will show them
what it is to be a thin crescent moon.
You and I unselfed, will be together,
indifferent to idle speculation, you and I.
The parrots of heaven will be cracking sugar
as we laugh together, you and I.
In one form upon this earth,
and in another form in a timeless sweet land.

A New Rule

It is the rule with drunkards to fall upon each other,
to quarrel, become violent, and make a scene.
The lover is even worse than a drunkard.
I will tell you what love is: to enter a mine of gold.
And what is that gold?
The lover is a king above all kings,
unafraid of death, not at all interested in a golden crown.
The dervish has a pearl concealed under his patched cloak.
Why should he go begging door to door?
Last night that moon came along,
drunk, dropping clothes in the street.
"Get up,"
I told my heart, "Give the soul a glass of wine.
The moment has come to join the nightingale in the garden,
to taste sugar with the soul-parrot."
I have fallen, with my heart shattered -
where else but on your path? And I
broke your bowl, drunk, my idol, so drunk,
don't let me be harmed, take my hand.
A new rule a new law has been born:
break all the glasses and fall toward the glassblower.

A Stone I Died

A stone I died and rose again a plant;
A plant I died and rose an animal;
I died an animal and was born a man.
Why should I fear? What have I lost by death?

All Through Eternity

All through eternity
Beauty unveils His exquisite form
in the solitude of nothingness;
He holds a mirror to His Face
and beholds His own beauty.
he is the knower and the known,
the seer and the seen;
No eye but His own
has ever looked upon this Universe.
His every quality finds an expression:
Eternity becomes the verdant field of Time and Space;
Love, the life-giving garden of this world.
Every branch and leaf and fruit
Reveals an aspect of His perfection-
They cypress give hint of His majesty,
The rose gives tidings of His beauty.
Whenever Beauty looks,
Love is also there;
Whenever beauty shows a rosy cheek
Love lights Her fire from that flame.
When beauty dwells in the dark folds of night
Love comes and finds a heart
entangled in tresses.
Beauty and Love are as body and soul.
Beauty is the mine, Love is the diamond.
They have together
since the beginning of time-
Side by side, step by step.

Any Lifetime

Any lifetime that is spent without seeing the master
Is either death in disguise or a deep sleep.
The water that pollutes you is poison;
The poison that purifies you is water.

Any Soul That Drank The Nectar
Any soul that drank the nectar of your passion was lifted.
From that water of life he is in a state of elation.
Death came, smelled me, and sensed your fragrance instead.
From then on, death lost all hope of me.

At the twilight, a moon appeared in the sky;
Then it landed on earth to look at me.
Like a hawk stealing a bird at the time of prey;
That moon stole me and rushed back into the sky.
I looked at myself, I did not see me anymore;
For in that moon, my body turned as fine as soul.
The nine spheres disappeared in that moon;
The ship of my existence drowned in that sea.

Bad Dreams

One day you will look back and laugh at yourself.
You'll say, ' I can't believe I was so asleep!
How did I ever forget the truth?
How ridiculous to believe that sadness and sickness
Are anything other than bad dreams.'

Be Lost In The Call

Lord, said David, since you do not need us,
why did you create these two worlds?
Reality replied: O prisoner of time,
I was a secret treasure of kindness and generosity,
and I wished this treasure to be known,
so I created a mirror: its shining face, the heart;
its darkened back, the world;
The back would please you if you've never seen the face.
Has anyone ever produced a mirror out of mud and straw?
Yet clean away the mud and straw,
and a mirror might be revealed.
Until the juice ferments a while in the cask,
it isn't wine. If you wish your heart to be bright,
you must do a little work.
My King addressed the soul of my flesh:
You return just as you left.
Where are the traces of my gifts?
We know that alchemy transforms copper into gold.
This Sun doesn't want a crown or robe from God's grace.
He is a hat to a hundred bald men,
a covering for ten who were naked.
Jesus sat humbly on the back of an ass, my child!
How could a zephyr ride an ass?
Spirit, find your way, in seeking lowness like a stream.
Reason, tread the path of selflessness into eternity.
Remember God so much that you are forgotten.
Let the caller and the called disappear;
be lost in the Call.

Be With Those Who Help Your Being

Be with those who help your being.
Don't sit with indifferent people, whose breath
comes cold out of their mouths.
Not these visible forms, your work is deeper.
A chunk of dirt thrown in the air breaks to pieces.
If you don't try to fly,
and so break yourself apart,
you will be broken open by death,
when it's too late for all you could become.
Leaves get yellow. The tree puts out fresh roots
and makes them green.
Why are you so content with a love that turns you yellow?

Because I Cannot Sleep

Because I cannot sleep
I make music at night.
I am troubled by the one
whose face has the color of spring flowers.
I have neither sleep nor patience,
neither a good reputation nor disgrace.
A thousand robes of wisdom are gone.
All my good manners have moved a thousand miles away.
The heart and the mind are left angry with each other.
The stars and the moon are envious of each other.
Because of this alienation the physical universe
is getting tighter and tighter.
The moon says, 'How long will I remain
suspended without a sun?'
Without Love's jewel inside of me,
let the bazaar of my existence be destroyed stone by stone.
O Love, You who have been called by a thousand names,
You who know how to pour the wine
into the chalice of the body,
You who give culture to a thousand cultures,
You who are faceless but have a thousand faces,
O Love, You who shape the faces
of Turks, Europeans, and Zanzibaris,
give me a glass from Your bottle,
or a handful of being from Your Branch.
Remove the cork once more.

Then we'll see a thousand chiefs prostrate themselves,
and a circle of ecstatic troubadours will play.
Then the addict will be freed of craving.
and will be resurrected,
and stand in awe till Judgement Day.

Behind The Scenes

Is it your face
that adorns the garden?
Is it your fragrance
that intoxicates this garden?
Is it your spirit
that has made this brook
a river of wine?
Hundreds have looked for you
and died searching
in this garden
where you hide behind the scenes.
But this pain is not for those
who come as lovers.
You are easy to find here.
You are in the breeze
and in this river of wine.

Birdsong

Birdsong brings relief
to my longing
I'm just as ecstatic as they are,
but with nothing to say!
Please universal soul, practice
some song or something through me!

Hearken to the reed-flute, how it complains,

Lamenting its banishment from its home:
'Ever since they tore me from my osier bed,
My plaintive notes have moved men and women to tears.
I burst my breast, striving to give vent to sighs,
And to express the pangs of my yearning for my home.
He who abides far away from his home
Is ever longing for the day he shall return.
My wailing is heard in every throng,
In concert with them that rejoice and them that weep.
Each interprets my notes in harmony with his own feelings,
But not one fathoms the secrets of my heart.
My secrets are not alien from my plaintive notes,
Yet they are not manifest to the sensual eye and ear.
Body is not veiled from soul, neither soul from body,
Yet no man hath ever seen a soul.'
This plaint of the flute is fire, not mere air.
Let him who lacks this fire be accounted dead!
'Tis the fire of love that inspires the flute,
'Tis the ferment of love that possesses the wine.
The flute is the confidant of all unhappy lovers;
Yea, its strains lay bare my inmost secrets.
Who hath seen a poison and an antidote like the flute?
Who hath seen a sympathetic consoler like the flute?
The flute tells the tale of love's bloodstained path,
It recounts the story of Majnun's love toils.
None is privy to these feelings save one distracted,
As ear inclines to the whispers of the tongue.
Through grief my days are as labor and sorrow,
My days move on, hand in hand with anguish.
Yet, though my days vanish thus, 'tis no matter,
Do thou abide, O Incomparable Pure One!

But all who are not fishes are soon tired of water;
And they who lack daily bread find the day very long;
So the 'Raw' comprehend not the state of the 'Ripe;'
Therefore it behoves me to shorten my discourse.
Arise, O son! burst thy bonds and be free!
How long wilt thou be captive to silver and gold?
Though thou pour the ocean into thy pitcher,
It can hold no more than one day's store.
The pitcher of the desire of the covetous never fills,
The oyster-shell fills not with pearls till it is content;
Only he whose garment is rent by the violence of love
Is wholly pure from covetousness and sin.
Hail to thee, then, O LOVE, sweet madness!
Thou who healest all our infirmities!
Who art the physician of our pride and self-conceit!
Who art our Plato and our Galen!
Love exalts our earthly bodies to heaven,
And makes the very hills to dance with joy!
O lover, 'twas love that gave life to Mount Sinai,
When 'it quaked, and Moses fell down in a swoon.'
Did my Beloved only touch me with his lips,
I too, like the flute, would burst out in melody.
But he who is parted from them that speak his tongue,
Though he possess a hundred voices, is perforce dumb.
When the rose has faded and the garden is withered,
The song of the nightingale is no longer to be heard.
The BELOVED is all in all, the lover only veils Him;
The BELOVED is all that lives, the lover a dead thing.
When the lover feels no longer LOVE's quickening,
He becomes like a bird who has lost its wings. Alas!
How can I retain my senses about me,

When the BELOVED shows not the light of His countenance?
LOVE desires that this secret should be revealed,
For if a mirror reflects not, of what use is it?
Knowest thou why thy mirror reflects not?
Because the rust has not been scoured from its face.
If it were purified from all rust and defilement,
It would reflect the shining of the SUN Of GOD.
O friends, ye have now heard this tale,
Which sets forth the very essence of my case.

Bring Wine

Bring wine, for I am suffering crop sickness from the vintage;
God has seized me, and I am thus held fast.
By love's soul, bring me a cup of wine that is the envy of the
sun, for I care aught but love.
Bring that which if I were to call it "soul" would be a shame,
for the reason that I am pained in the head because of the soul.
Bring that whose name is not contained in this mouth, through
which the fissures of my speech split asunder.
Bring that which, when it is not present, I am stupid and ignorant,
but when I am with it, I am the king of the subtle and
crafty ones.
Bring that which, the moment it is void of my head, I become
black and dark, you might say I am of the infidels.
Bring that which delivers out of this "bring" and "do not
bring"; bring quickly, and repel me not, saying, "Whence shall
I bring it?"

Bring, and deliver the roof of the heavens through the long
night from my abundant smoke and lamentations.
Bring that which after my death, even out of my dust, will
restore me to speech and thanksgiving even as Najjar.
Bring me wine, for I am guardian of wine like a goblet, for
whatever has gone into my stomach I deliver back completely.
Najjar said, "After my death would that my people might be
open-eyed to the ecstasy within me.
"They would not regard my bones and blood; in spirit I ama
mighty king, even though in body I am vile.
"What a ladder I, the Carpenter, have chiseled! My going has
reached the roof of the seventh heaven.
"I journeyed like the Messiah, my ass remained below; I do
no grieve for my ass, nor am I asslike of ears.
"Do not like Eblis see in Adam only water and clay; see that
behind the clay are my hundred thousand rose bowers."
Shams-e Tabrizi rose up from this flesh saying, " I am the
sun. Bring up my head from this mire.
"Err not, when I enter the mire once more, for I am at rest,
and am ashamed of this veil.
"Every morning I will rise up, despite the blind; for the sake
of the blind I will not cease to rise and set."

Come, Come, Whoever You Are

Wonderer, worshipper, lover of leaving.
It doesn't matter.
Ours is not a caravan of despair.
Come, even if you have broken your vow
a thousand times
Come, yet again, come, come.

Confused And Distraught

Again I am raging,
I am in such a state by your soul that every
bond you bind, I break, by your soul.
I am like heaven, like the moon, like a candle by your glow;
I am all reason, all love, all soul, by your soul.
My joy is of your doing, my hangover of your thorn;
whatever side you turn your face,
I turn mine, by your soul.
I spoke in error;
it is not surprising to speak in error in this state,
for this moment I cannot tell cup from wine, by your soul.
I am that madman in bonds who binds the
'divs'; I, the madman,am a Solomon with the 'divs', by your soul.
Whatever form other than love raises up its head from my
heart, forthwith I drive it out of the court of my heart,
by your soul.
Come, you who have departed, for the thing that departs
comes back; neither you are that,
by my soul, nor I am that, by your soul.
Disbeliever, do not conceal disbelief in your soul,
for I will recite the secret of your destiny, by your soul.
Out of love of Sham-e Tabrizi,
through wakefulness or nightrising,
like a spinning mote I am distraught, by your soul.

Defeated By Love

The sky was lit
by the splendor of the moon
So powerful
I fell to the ground
Your love
has made me sure
I am ready to forsake
this worldly life
and surrender
to the magnificence
of your Being

Description Of Love

A true lover is proved such by his pain of heart;
No sickness is there like sickness of heart.
The lover's ailment is different from all ailments;
Love is the astrolabe of God's mysteries.
A lover may hanker after this love or that love,
But at the last he is drawn to the KING of love.
However much we describe and explain love,
When we fall in love we are ashamed of our words.
Explanation by the tongue makes most things clear,
But love unexplained is clearer.
When pen hasted to write,
On reaching the subject of love it split in twain.
When the discourse touched on the matter of love,
Pen was broken and paper torn.
In explaining it Reason sticks fast, as an ass in mire;
Naught but Love itself can explain love and lovers!
None but the sun can display the sun,
If you would see it displayed, turn not away from it.
Shadows, indeed, may indicate the sun's presence,
But only the sun displays the light of life.
Shadows induce slumber, like evening talks,
But when the sun arises the 'moon is split asunder.'
In the world there is naught so wondrous as the sun,

But the Sun of the soul sets not and has no yesterday.
Though the material sun is unique and single,
We can conceive similar suns like to it.
But the Sun of the soul, beyond this firmament,
No like thereof is seen in concrete or abstract.
Where is there room in conception for His essence,
So that similitudes of HIM should be conceivable?

Did I Not Say To You

Did I not say to you, "Go not there, for I am your friend; in this
mirage of annihilation I am the fountain of life? "
Even though in anger you depart a hundred thousand years
from me, in the end you will come to me, for I am your goal.
Did I not say to you, "Be not content with worldly forms, for I
am the fashioner of the tabernacle of your contentment? "
Did I not say to you, "I am the sea and you are a single fish;
go not to dry land, for I am your crystal sea? "
Did I not say to you, " Go not like birds to the snare; come, for
I am the power of flight and your wings and feet? "
Did I not say to you, " They will waylay you and make you
cold, for I am the fire and warmth and heat of your desire? "
Did I not say to you, " They will implant in you ugly qualities
so that you will forget that I am the source of purity to you? "
Did I not say to you, "Do not say from what direction the servant's
affairs come into order? " I am the Creator without directions.
If you are the lamp of the heart, know where the road is to the
house; and if you are godlike of attribute, know that I am your
Master.

Do You Love Me?

A lover asked his beloved,
Do you love yourself more
than you love me?
The beloved replied,
I have died to myself
and I live for you.
I've disappeared from myself
and my attributes.
I am present only for you.
I have forgotten all my learning,
but from knowing you
I have become a scholar.
I have lost all my strength,
but from your power
I am able.
If I love myself
I love you.
If I love you
I love myself.

Draw It Now From Eternity's Jar

Come, come, awaken all true drunkards!
Pour the wine that is Life itself!
O cupbearer of the Eternal Wine,
Draw it now from Eternity's Jar!
This wine doesn't run down the throat
But it looses torrents of words!
Cupbearer, make my soul fragrant as musk,
This noble soul of mine that knows the Invisible!
Pour out the wine for the morning drinkers!
Pour them this subtle and priceless musk!
Pass it around to everyone in the assembly
In the cups of your blazing drunken eyes!
Pass a philter from your eyes to everyone else's
In a way the mouth knows nothing of,
For this is the way cupbearers always offer
The holy and mysterious wine to lovers.
Hurry, the eyes of every atom in Creation
Are famished for this flaming-out of splendour!
Procure for yourself this fragrance of musk
And with it split open the breast of heaven!
The waves of the fragrance of this musk
Drive all Josephs out of their minds forever!

Every Day I Bear A Burden

Every day I bear a burden, and I bear this calamity for a purpose:
I bear the discomfort of cold and
December's snow in hope of spring.
Before the fattener-up of all who are lean,
 I drag this so emaciated body;
Though they expel me from two hundred cities,
 I bear it for the sake of the love of a prince;
Though my shop and house be laid waste,
I bear it in fidelity to a tulip bed.
God's love is a very strong fortress;
I carry my soul's baggage inside a fortress.
I bear the arrogance of every stonehearted
stranger for the sake of a friend, of one long-suffering;
For the sake of his ruby I dig out mountains and mine;
for the sake of that roseladen one I endure a thorn.
For the sake of those two intoxicating eyes of his, like
the intoxicated I endure crop sickness;

For the sake of a quarry not to be contained in a snare, I spread out
the snare and decoy of the hunter.
He said, "Will you bear this sorrow till the Resurrection?"
Yes, Friend, I bear it, I bear it.
My breast is the Cave and Shams-e
Tabrizi is the Companion of the Cave.

Ghazal 119

I don't need
a companion who is
nasty sad and sour
the one who is
like a grave
dark depressing and bitter
a sweetheart is a mirror
a friend a delicious cake
it isn't worth spending
an hour with anyone else
a companion who is
in love only with the self
has five distinct characters
stone hearted
unsure of every step
lazy and disinterested
keeping a poisonous face
the more this companion waits around
the more bitter everything will get
just like a vinegar
getting more sour with time
enough is said about
sour and bitter faces
a heart filled with desire for
sweetness and tender souls
must not waste itself with unsavory matters

Ghazal

You who are not kept anxiously awake for love's sake, sleep on.
In restless search for that river, we hurry along;
you whose heart such anxiety has not disturbed, sleep on.
Love's place is out beyond the many separate sects;
since you love choosing and excluding, sleep on.
Love's dawn cup is our sunrise, his dusk our supper;
you whose longing is for sweets and whose passion is for supper,
sleep on.
In search of the philosopher's stone, we are melting like copper;
you whose philosopher's stone is cushion and pillow, sleep on.
I have abandoned hope for my brain and head; you who wish for
a clear head and fresh brain, sleep on.
I have torn speech like a tattered robe and let words go;
you who are still dressed in your clothes, sleep on.

Ghazal Of Rumi

I was dead, then alive.
Weeping, then laughing.
The power of love came into me,
and I became fierce like a lion,
then tender like the evening star.
He said, 'You're not mad enough.
You don't belong in this house.'
I went wild and had to be tied up.
He said, 'Still not wild enough
to stay with us!'
I broke through another layer
into joyfulness.
He said, 'Its not enough.'
I died.

Here I Am

All night, a man called 'Allah'
Until his lips were bleeding.
Then the Devil said, 'Hey! Mr Gullible!
How comes you've been calling all night
And never once heard Allah say, 'Here, I am'?
You call out so earnestly and, in reply, what?
I'll tell you what. Nothing!'
The man suddenly felt empty and abandoned.
Depressed, he threw himself on the ground
And fell into a deep sleep.
In a dream, he met Abraham, who asked,
'Why are you regretting praising Allah?'
The man said, ' I called and called
But Allah never replied, 'Here I am.'
Abraham explained, 'Allah has said,
'Your calling my name is My reply.
Your longing for Me is My message to you.
All your attempts to reach Me
Are in reality My attempts to reach you.
Your fear and love are a noose to catch Me.
In the silence surrounding every call of 'Allah'
Waits a thousand replies of 'Here I am.'

How Long

How long will you think about this painful life?
How long will you think about this harmful world?
The only thing it can take from you is your body.
Don't say all this rubbish and stop thinking.

I Am A Sculptor, A Molder Of Form

I am a sculptor, a molder of form.
In every moment I shape an idol.
But then, in front of you, I melt them down
I can rouse a hundred forms
and fill them with spirit,
but when I look into your face,
I want to throw them in the fire.
My souls spills into yours and is blended.
Because my soul has absorbed your fragrance,
I cherish it.
Every drop of blood I spill
informs the earth,
I merge with my Beloved
when I participate in love.
In this house of mud and water,
my heart has fallen to ruins.
Enter this house, my Love, or let me leave.

I Am And I Am Not

I'm drenched
in the flood
which has yet to come
I'm tied up
in the prison
which has yet to exist
Not having played
the game of chess
I'm already the checkmate
Not having tasted
a single cup of your wine
I'm already drunk
Not having entered
the battlefield
I'm already wounded and slain
I no longer
know the difference
between image and reality
Like the shadow
I am
And
I am not
Translated by: Fereydoun Kia

I Am Only The House Of Your Beloved

'I am only the house of your beloved,
not the beloved herself:
true love is for the treasure,
not for the coffer that contains it.'
The real beloved is that one who is unique,
who is your beginning and your end.
When you find that one,
you'll no longer expect anything else:
that is both the manifest and the mystery.
That one is the lord of states of feeling,
dependent on none;
month and year are slaves to that moon.
When he bids the 'state,'
it does His bidding;
when that one wills, bodies become spirit.

I Am Part Of The Load

I am part of the load
Not rightly balanced
I drop off in the grass,
like the old Cave-sleepers, to browse
wherever I fall.
For hundreds of thousands of years I have been dust-grains
floating and flying in the will of the air,
often forgetting ever being
in that state, but in sleep
I migrate back. I spring loose
from the four-branched, time -and-space cross,
this waiting room.
I walk into a huge pasture
I nurse the milk of millennia
Everyone does this in different ways.
Knowing that conscious decisions
and personal memory
are much too small a place to live,
every human being streams at night into the loving nowhere, or
during the day,in some absorbing work.

I Closed My Eyes To Creation

I closed my eyes to creation when I beheld his beauty, I became
intoxicated with his beauty and bestowed my soul.
For the sake of Solomon's seal I became wax in all my body,
and in order to become illumined I rubbed my wax.
I saw his opinion and cast away my own twisted opinion; I
became his reed pipe and likewise lamented on his lip.
He was in my hand, and blindly I groped for him with my
hand; I was in his hand, and yet I inquired of those who were
misinformed.
I must have been either a simpleton or drunk or mad that
fearfully I was stealing from my own gold.
Like a thief I crept through a crack in the wall into my own
vine, like a thief I gathered jasmine from my own garden.
Enough, do not twist my secret upon your fingertips, for I have
twisted off out of your twisted fist.
Shams-e Tabriz, from whom comes the light of moon and
stars—though I am grieving with sorrow for him, I am like the
crescent of the festival.

I Have A Fire For You In My Mouth

I have a fire for you in my mouth, but I have a hundred seals
on my tongue.
The flames which I have in my heart would make one mouthful
of both worlds.
Though the entire world should pass away, without the world
I possess the kingdom of a hundred worlds.
Caravans which are loaded with sugar I have in motion for
the Egypt of nonexistence.
The drunkenness of love makes me unaware whether I have
profit of loss therefrom.
The body's eye was scattering pearls because of love, till now
I have a pearl-scattering soul.
I am not housebound, for like Jesus I have a home in the fourth
Heaven.
Thanks be to Him who gives soul to the body; if the soul
should depart, yet I have the soul of the soul.
Seek from me that which Shams-e Tabrizi has bestowed, for
I have the same.

I Have A Fire For You In My Mouth

I have a fire for you in my mouth, but I have a hundred seals
on my tongue.
The flames which I have in my heart would make one mouthful
of both worlds.
Though the entire world should pass away, without the world
I possess the kingdom of a hundred worlds.
Caravans which are loaded with sugar I have in motion for
the Egypt of nonexistence.
The drunkenness of love makes me unaware whether I have
profit of loss therefrom.
The body's eye was scattering pearls because of love, till now
I have a pearl-scattering soul.
I am not housebound, for like Jesus I have a home in the fourth
Heaven.
Thanks be to Him who gives soul to the body; if the soul
should depart, yet I have the soul of the soul.
Seek from me that which Shams-e Tabrizi has bestowed, for
I have the same.

I Have Been Tricked By Flying Too Close
I have been tricked by flying too close
to what I thought I loved.
Now the candleflame is out, the wine spilled,
and the lovers have withdrawn
somewhere beyond my squinting.
The amount I thought I'd won, I've lost.
My prayers becomes bitter and all about blindness.
How wonderful it was to be for a while
with those who surrender.
Others only turn their faces on way,
then another, like pigeon in flight.
I have known pigeons who fly in a nowhere,
and birds that eat grainlessness,
and tailor who sew beautiful clothes
by tearing them to pieces.

I Have Fallen Into Unconsciousness

I have got out of my own control,
I have fallen into unconsciousness; in my utter
unconsciousness how joyful I am with myself!
The darling sewed up my eyes so that
I might not see other than him, so that
suddenly I opened my eyes on his face.
My soul fought with me saying,
"Do not pain me"; I said, "Take your divorce."
She said, "Grant it"; I granted it.
When my mother saw on my cheek the brand of your love she cut
my umbilical cord on that, the moment I was born.
If I travel to heaven and read the Tablet of the Unseen, O you who
are my soul's salvation, without you how I am ruined!
When you cast aside the veil the dead become alive; the light of your
face reminded me of the Covenant of Alast.
When I became lost, O soul, through love of the king
of the peris, hidden from self and creatures,
I am as if peri-born myself.
I said to the Tabriz of Shams-e Din,
"O body, what are you?" Body said, "Earth";
Soul said, "I am distraught like the wind."

I See So Deeply Within Myself
I see so deeply within myself.
Not needing my eyes, I can see everything clearly.
Why would I want to bother my eyes again
Now that I see the world through His eyes?

I Swear

I swear, since seeing Your face,
the whole world is fraud and fantasy
The garden is bewildered as to what is leaf
or blossom. The distracted birds
can't distinguish the birdseed from the snare.
A house of love with no limits,
a presence more beautiful than venus or the moon,
a beauty whose image fills the mirror of the heart.

I Throw It All Away

You play with the great globe of union,
you that see everyone so clearly
and cannot be seen. Even universal
intelligence gets blurry when it thinks
you may leave. You came here alone,
but you create hundreds of new worlds.
Spring is a peacock flirting with
revelation. The rose gardens flame.
Ocean enters the boat. I throw
it all away, except this love for Shams.
Translation by: Coleman Barks

I Was Dead

i was dead
i came alive
i was tears
i became laughter
all because of love
when it arrived
my temporal life
from then on
changed to eternal
love said to me
you are not
crazy enough
you don't
fit this house
i went and
became crazy
crazy enough
to be in chains
love said
you are not
intoxicated enough
you don't
fit the group
i went and
got drunk
drunk enough
to overflow
with light-headedness
love said
you are still
too clever
filled with
imagination and skepticism

i went and
became gullible and in fright
pulled away from it all love said
you are a candle
attracting everyone
gathering every one
around you
i am no more
a candle spreading light
i gather no more crowds
and like smoke
i am all scattered now
love said
you are a teacher
you are a head
and for everyone
you are a leader
i am no more
not a teacher
not a leader
just a servant
to your wishes
love said
you already have
your own wings
i will not give you
more feathers
and then my heart
pulled itself apart
and filled to the brim
with a new light
overflowed with fresh life
now even the heavens
are thankful that
because of love
i have become
the giver of light

I Will Beguile Him With The Tongue

Reason says, " I will beguile him with the tongue."; Love says,
"Be silent. I will beguile him with the soul."
The soul says to the heart, "Go, do not laugh at me and yourself.
What is there that is not his, that I may beguile him
thereby?"
He is not sorrowful and anxious and seeking oblivion that I
may beguile him with wine and a heavy measure.
The arrow of his glance needs not a bow that I should beguile
the shaft of his gaze with a bow.
He is not prisoner of the world, fettered to this world of earth,
that I should beguile him with gold of the kingdom of the world.
He is an angel, though in form he is a man; he is not lustful
that I should beguile him with women.
Angels start away from the house wherein this form is, so how
should I beguile him with such a form and likeness?
He does not take a flock of horses, since he flies on wings; his
food is light, so how should I beguile him with bread?

He is not a merchant and trafficker in the market of the world
that I should beguile him with enchantment of grain and loss.
He is not veiled that I should make myself out sick and utter
sighs, to beguile him with lamentation.
I will bind my head and bow my head, for I have got out of
hand; I will not beguile his compassion with sickness or fluttering.
Hair by hair he sees my crookedness and feigning; what's
hidden from him that I should beguile him with anything hidden.
He is not a seeker of fame, a prince addicted to poets, that I
should beguile him with verses and lyrics and flowing poetry.
The glory of the unseen form is too great for me to beguile it
with blessing or Paradise.
Shams-e Tabriz, who is his chosen and beloved–perchance I
will beguile him with this same pole of the age.

If A Tree Could Wander

Oh, if a tree could wander
and move with foot and wings!
It would not suffer the axe blows
and not the pain of saws!
For would the sun not wander
away in every night ?
How could at ev'ry morning
the world be lighted up?
And if the ocean's water
would not rise to the sky,
How would the plants be quickened
by streams and gentle rain?
The drop that left its homeland,
the sea, and then returned ?
It found an oyster waiting
and grew into a pearl.
Did Yusaf not leave his father,
in grief and tears and despair?
Did he not, by such a journey,
gain kingdom and fortune wide?
Did not the Prophet travel
to far Medina, friend?
And there he found a new kingdom
and ruled a hundred lands.
You lack a foot to travel?
Then journey into yourself!
And like a mine of rubies
receive the sunbeams? print!
Out of yourself ? such a journey
will lead you to your self,

It leads to transformation
of dust into pure gold!

If I Weep

If I weep, if I come with excuses,
my beloved puts cotton wool in his ears.
Every cruelty which he commits becomes him, every cruelty which
he commits I endure.
If he accounts me nonexistent, I account his tyranny generosity.
The cure of the ache of my heart is the ache for him; how shall I not
surrender my heart to his ache?
Only then are glory and respect mine,
when his glorious love renders me contemptible.
Only then does the vine of my body become wine, when the wine-
presser stamps on me and spurns me underfoot.
I yield my soul like grapes under the trampling,
that my secret heart may make merry,
Though the grapes weep only blood, for
I am vexed with this cruelty and tyranny.
He who pounds upon me puts cotton wool in his ears saying,
"I do not press unwittingly.
If you disbelieve, you are excusable, but
I am the Abu'l Hikam [the expert] in this affair.
When you burst under the labor of my feet,
then you will render much thanks to me."

If You Show Patience

If you show patience, I'll rid you of this virtue.
If you fall asleep, I'll rub the sleep from your eyes.
If you become a mountain, I'll melt you in fire.
And if you become an ocean, I'll drink all your water.
If You Want What Visible Reality
If you want what visible reality
can give, you're an employee.
If you want the unseen world,
you're not living your truth.
Both wishes are foolish,
but you'll be forgiven for forgetting
that what you really want is
love's confusing joy.

In Love

In love, aside from sipping the wine of timelessness,
nothing else exists.
There is no reason for living except for giving one's life.
I said, 'First I know you, then I die.'
He said, 'For the one who knows Me, there is no dying.'

In The Arc Of Your Mallet

Don't go anywhere without me.
Let nothing happen in the sky apart from me,
or on the ground, in this world or that world,
without my being in its happening.
Vision, see nothing I don't see.
Language, say nothing.
The way the night knows itself with the moon,
be that with me. Be the rose
nearest to the thorn that I am.
I want to feel myself in you when you taste food,
in the arc of your mallet when you work,
when you visit friends, when you go
up on the roof by yourself at night.
There's nothing worse than to walk out along the street
without you. I don't know where I'm going.
You're the road, and the knower of roads,
more than maps, more than love

In The End

In the end, the mountains of imagination were nothing
but a house.
And this grand life of mine was nothing but an excuse.
You've been hearing my story so patiently for a lifetime
Now hear this: it was nothing but a fairy tale.
In The Waters Of Purity
In the waters of purity, I melted like salt
Neither blasphemy, nor faith, nor conviction, nor
doubt remained.
In the center of my heart a star has appeared
And all the seven heavens have become lost in it.

Laila And The Khalifa.

The Khalifa said to Laila, "Art thou really she
For whom Majnun lost his head and went distracted?
Thou art not fairer than many other fair ones."
She replied, "Be silent; thou art not Majnun!"
If thou hadst Majnun's eyes,
The two worlds would be within thy view.
Thou art in thy senses, but Majnun is beside himself.
In love to be wide awake is treason.
The more a man is awake, the more he sleeps (to love);
His (critical) wakefulness is worse than slumbering.
Our wakefulness fetters our spirits,
Then our souls are a prey to divers whims,
Thoughts of loss and gain and fears of misery.
They retain not purity, nor dignity, nor lustre,
Nor aspiration to soar heavenwards.
That one is really sleeping who hankers after each whim
And holds parley with each fancy.

Last Night My Soul Cried
O Exalted Sphere Of Heaven

Last night my soul cried, "O exalted sphere of Heaven, you hang
indeed inverted,with flames in your belly.
"Without sin and crime, eternally revolving upon your body in its
complaining is the indigo of mourning;
"Now happy, now unhappy, like Abraham in the fire; at once king
and beggar like Ebrahim-e Adham.
"In your form you are terrifying, yet your state is full of anguish: you
turn round like a millstone and writhe like a snake."
Heaven the blessed replied,
"How should I not fear that one who makes the
Paradise of the world as Hell?
"In his hand earth is as wax, he makes it Zangi and Rumi , he makes
it falcon and owl, he makes it sugar and poison.

"He is hidden, friend, and has set us forth thus patent so that he may become concealed.

"How should the ocean of the world be concealed under straws? The straws have been set adancing, the waves tumbling up and down'

"Your body is like the land floating on the waters of the soul; your soul is veiled in the body alike in wedding feast or sorrow.

"In the veil you are a new bride, hot-tempered and obstinate; he is railing sweetly at the good and the bad of the world.

"Through him the earth is a green meadow, the heavens are unresting; on every side through him a fortunate one pardoned and preserved.

"Reason a seeker of certainty through him, patience a seeker of help through him, love seeing the unseen through him, earth taking the form of Adam through him.

"Air seeking and searching, water hand-washing, we Messiah-like speaking, earth Mary-like silent.

"Behold the sea with its billows circling round the earthy ship; behold Kaabas and Meccas at the bottom of this well of Zamzam!"

The king says, "Be silent, do not cast yourself into the well, for you do not know how to make a bucket and a rope out of my withered stumps.

Last Night You Left Me And Slept

Last night you left me and slept
your own deep sleep. Tonight you turn
and turn. I say,
'You and I will be together
till the universe dissolves.'
You mumble back things you thought of
when you were drunk.

Late, By Myself

Late, by myself, in the boat of myself,
no light and no land anywhere,
cloudcover thick. I try to stay
just above the surface,
yet I'm already under
and living with the ocean

Let Go Of Your Worries

Let go of your worries
and be completely clear-hearted,
like the face of a mirror
that contains no images.
If you want a clear mirror,
behold yourself
and see the shameless truth,
which the mirror reflects.
If metal can be polished
to a mirror-like finish,
what polishing might the mirror
of the heart require?
Between the mirror and the heart
is this single difference:
the heart conceals secrets,
while the mirror does not.

Let Me Be Mad

O incomparable Giver of life, cut reason loose at last!
Let it wander grey-eyed from vanity to vanity.
Shatter open my skull, pour in it the wine of madness!
Let me be mad, as You; mad with You, with us.
Beyond the sanity of fools is a burning desert
Where Your sun is whirling in every atom:
Beloved, drag me there, let me roast in Perfection!

Light Breeze

As regards feeling pain, like a hand cut in battle,
consider the body a robe you wear.
When you meet someone you love, do you kiss their clothes?
Search out who's inside.
Union with God is sweeter than body comforts.
We have hands and feet different from these.
Sometimes in dream we see them.
That is not illusion. It's seeing truly. You do have a spirit body;
don't dread leaving the physical one.
Sometimes someone feels this truth so
strongly that he or she can live in mountain solitude totally refreshed.
The worried, heroic doings of men and women seem weary and
futile to dervishes enjoying the light breeze of spirit.

Light Up The Fire

I gaze into the heart, lowly it may be,
Thought the words be higher still.
For the heart is all the substance,
The speech an accident.
How many phrases will you speak,
Too many for me.
How much burning, burning will you feel,
Be friendly with the fire, enough for me.
Light up the fire of love inside,
And blaze the thoughts away.

Like This

If anyone asks you
how the perfect satisfaction
of all our sexual wanting
will look, lift your face
and say, Like this.
When someone mentions the gracefulness
of the nightsky, climb up on the roof
and dance and say, Like this.
If anyone wants to know what 'spirit' is,
or what 'God's fragrance' means,
lean your head toward him or her.
Keep your face there close. Like this.
When someone quotes the old poetic image
about clouds gradually uncovering the moon,
slowly loosen knot by knot the strings
of your robe. Like this.
If anyone wonders how Jesus raised the dead,
don't try to explain the miracle.
Kiss me on the lips.
Like this. Like this.
When someone asks what it means
to 'die for love,' point here.
If someone asks how tall I am, frown
and measure with your fingers the space
between the creases on your forehead.
This tall.
The soul sometimes leaves the body, the returns.
When someone doesn't believe that,

walk back into my house.
Like this.
When lovers moan,
they're telling our story.
Like this.
I am a sky where spirits live.
Stare into this deepening blue,
while the breeze says a secret.
Like this.
When someone asks what there is to do,
light the candle in his hand.
Like this.
How did Joseph's scent come to Jacob?
Huuuuu.
How did Jacob's sight return?
Huuuu.
A little wind cleans the eyes.
Like this.
When Shams comes back from Tabriz,
he'll put just his head around the edge
of the door to surprise us
Like this.

Lord, What A Beloved Is Mine!

Lord, what a Beloved is mine! I have a sweet quarry; I possess
in my breast a hundred meadows from his reed.
When in anger the messenger comes and repairs towards me,
he says, "Whither are you fleeing? I have business with you."
Last night I asked the new moon concerning my Moon. The
moon said, "I am running in his wake, my foot is in his dust."
When the sun arose I said," How yellow of face you are!" The
sun said, "Out of shame for his countenance I have a face of gold."
"Water, you are prostrate, you are running on your head and
face." Water said, "Because of his incantation I move like a snake."
"Noble fire, why do you writhe so?" Fire said, "Because of
the lightning of his face my heart is restless."
"Wind-messenger of the world, why are you light of heart?"
Wind said, "My heart would burn if the choice were mine."
"Earth, what are you meditation, silent and watchful?" Earth
said, "Within me I have a garden and spring."
Pass over these elements, God is our succorer; my head is
aching, in my hand I hold wine.
If you have barred sleep to us,
the way of intoxication is open.
Since I have one to assist,
he offers wine in both hands.
Be silent, that without this tongue
the heart may speak; when
I hear the speech of the heart,
I feel ashamed of this speech.

Love

Are you fleeing from Love because of a single humiliation?
What do you know of Love except the name?
Love has a hundred forms of pride and disdain,
and is gained by a hundred means of persuasion.
Since Love is loyal, it purchases one who is loyal:
it has no interest in a disloyal companion.
The human being resembles a tree; its root is a covenant with God:
that root must be cherished with all one's might.
A weak covenant is a rotten root, without grace or fruit.
Though the boughs and leaves of the date palm are green,
greenness brings no benefit if the root is corrupt.
If a branch is without green leaves, yet has a good root,
a hundred leaves will put forth their hands in the end.

Love And Imagination

Love and imagination are magicians
Who create an image of the Beloved in your mind
With which you share your secret intimate moments.
This apparition is made of nothing at al,
But from its mouth comes the question,
'Am I not your Loved One?'
and from you the soft reply'.'

Love Has Nothing To Do With The Five Senses

Love has nothing to do with
the five senses and the six directions:
its goal is only to experience
the attraction exerted by the Beloved.
Afterwards, perhaps, permission
will come from God:
the secrets that ought to be told will be told
with an eloquence nearer to the understanding
of these subtle confusing allusions.
The secret is partner with none
but the knower of the secret:
in the skeptic's ear
the secret is no secret at all.

Love Is Reckless

Love is reckless; not reason.
Reason seeks a profit.
Love comes on strong,
consuming herself, unabashed.
Yet, in the midst of suffering,
Love proceeds like a millstone,
hard surfaced and straightforward.
Having died of self-interest,
she risks everything and asks for nothing.
Love gambles away every gift God bestows.
Without cause God gave us Being;
without cause, give it back again.

Love Is The Cure

for your pain will keep giving birth to more pain
until your eyes constantly exhale love
as effortlessly as your body yields its scent.'

Love Is The Water Of Life

Everything other than love for the most beautiful God
though it be sugar- eating.
What is agony of the spirit?
To advance toward death without seizing
hold of the Water of Life.

Love Makes

Love makes bitter things sweet.
Love turns copper to gold.
With love dregs settle into clarity.
With love suffering ceases.
Love brings the dead back to life.
Love transforms the King into a slave.
Love is the consummation of Gnosis.
How could a fool sit on such a throne?

Lovers

O lovers, lovers it is time
to set out from the world.
I hear a drum in my soul's ear
coming from the depths of the stars.
Our camel driver is at work;
the caravan is being readied.
He asks that we forgive him
for the disturbance he has caused us,
He asks why we travelers are asleep.
Everywhere the murmur of departure;
the stars, like candles
thrust at us from behind blue veils,
and as if to make the invisible plain,
a wondrous people have come forth.

Masnawi

In the prologue to the Masnavi Rumi hailed Love and its sweet madness that heals all infirmities, and he exhorted the reader to burst the bonds to silver and gold to be free. The Beloved is all in all and is only veiled by the lover. Rumi identified the first cause of all things as God and considered all second causes subordinate to that. Human minds recognize the second causes, but only prophets perceive the action of the first cause. One story tells of a clever rabbit who warned the lion about another lion and showed the lion his own image in a well, causing him to attack it and drown. After delivering his companions from the tyrannical lion, the rabbit urges them to engage in the more difficult warfare against their own inward lusts. In a debate between trusting God and human exertion, Rumi quoted the prophet Muhammad as saying, "Trust in God, yet tie the camel's leg."8 He also mentioned the adage that the worker is the friend of God; so in trusting in providence one need not neglect to use means. Exerting oneself can be giving thanks for God's blessings; but he asked if fatalism shows gratitude.

God is hidden and has no opposite,
not seen by us yet seeing us. Form is born of
the formless but ultimately returns to the formless. An arrow shot by God cannot remain in the air but must return to God. Rumi reconciled God's agency with human free will and found the divine voice in the inward voice. Those in close communion with God are free, but the one who does not love is fettered by compulsion. God is the agency and first cause of our actions, but human will as the second cause finds recompense in hell or with the Friend. God is like the soul, and the world is like the body.

The good and evil of bodies comes from souls. When the sanctuary of true prayer is revealed to one, it is shameful to turn back to mere formal religion. Rumi confirmed Muhammad's view that women hold dominion over the wise and men of heart; but violent fools, lacking tenderness, gentleness, and friendship, try to hold the upper hand over women, because they are swayed by their animal nature. The human qualities of love and tenderness can control the animal passions. Rumi concluded that woman is a ray of God and the Creator's self.

When the Light of God illumines the inner person, one is freed from effects and has no need of signs for the assurance of love. Beauty busies itself with a mirror.

Since not being is the mirror of being, the wise choose the self-abnegation of not being so that being may be displayed in that not being. The wealthy show their liberality on the poor, and the hungry are the mirror of bread. Those recognizing and confessing their defects are hastening toward perfection; but whoever considers oneself perfect already is not advancing. The poet suggested driving out this sickness of arrogance with tears from the heart. The fault of the devil (Iblis) was in thinking himself better than others, and the same weakness lurks in the soul of all creatures. Heart knowledge bears people up in friendship, but body knowledge weighs them down with burdens.

Rumi wrote how through love all things become better. Doing kindness is the game of the good, who seek to alleviate suffering in the world.

Wherever there is a pain, a remedy is sent. Call on God so that the love of God may manifest. Rumi recommended the proverb that the moral way is not to find fault with others but to be admonished by their bad example. The mosque built in the hearts of the saints is the place for all worship, for God dwells there. Rumi began the third book of his Masnavi as follows:
In the Name of God the Compassionate, the Merciful.
The sciences of (Divine) Wisdom are God's armies, wherewith He strengthens the spirits of the initiates, and purifies their knowledge from the defilement of ignorance, their justice from the defilement of iniquity, their generosity from the defilement of ostentation, and their forbearance from the defilement of foolishness; and brings near to them whatever was far from them in respect of the understanding of the state hereafter; and makes easy to them whatever was hard to them in respect of obedience (to Him) and zealous endeavor (to serve Him).

A sage warns travelers that if they kill a baby elephant to eat, its parents will probably track them down and kill them; yet they do so, although one refrains from the killing and eating. As they sleep, a huge elephant smells their breath and kills all those who had eaten the young elephant but spares the one who had abstained. From foul breath the stench of pride, lust, and greed rises to heaven.

Pain may be better than dominion in the world so that one may call on God in secret; the cries of the sorrowful come from burning hearts. Rumi also told the story of the Hindus feeling the different parts of an elephant in a dark room. He emphasized that in substance all religions are one and the same, because all praises are directed to God's light. They err only because they have mistaken opinions. Sinners and criminals betray themselves especially in times of passion and angry talk. Prophets warn you of hidden dangers the worldly cannot see.

Humans have the ability to engage in any action, but for Rumi worship of God is the main object of human existence.

Rumi wrote that Sufism is to find joy in the heart whenever distress and care assail it. He believed the power of choice is like capital yielding profit, but he advised us to remember well the day of final accounting. Many of his stories are designed to show the difference between what is self-evident by experience and what is inferred through the authority of others. His philosophy of evolution of consciousness is encapsulated in the following verses:

I died as inanimate matter and arose a plant,
I died as a plant and rose again an animal.
I died as an animal and arose a man.
Why then should I fear to become less by dying?
I shall die once again as a man
To rise an angel perfect from head to foot!
Again when I suffer dissolution as an angel,
I shall become what passes the conception of man!
Let me then become non-existent, for non-existence
Sings to me in organ tones, "To him shall we return."

When the love of God arises in your heart, without doubt God also feels love for you. The soul loves wisdom, knowledge, and exalted things; but the body desires
houses, gardens, vineyards, food, and material goods. Rumi also believed that there is no absolute bad; the evils in the world are only relative. A serpent's poison protects its own life; but in relation to a person it can mean death. When what is hateful leads you to your beloved, it immediately becomes agreeable to you. Solomon built the temple by hiring workers, for humans can be controlled by money.

Men are as demons, and lust of wealth their chain,
Which drags them forth to toil in shop and field.
This chain is made of their fears and anxieties.
Deem not that these men have no chain upon them.
It causes them to engage in labor and the chase,
It forces them to toil in mines and on the sea,
It urges them towards good and towards evil.
Rumi warned against bad friends who can be like weeds in the temple of the heart; for if a liking for bad friends grows in you, they can subvert you and your temple. He also warned against the judges who confine their view to externals and base their decisions on outward appearances; these heretics have secretly shed the blood of many believers. Partial reason cannot see beyond the grave; but true reason looks beyond to the day of judgment and thus is able to steer a better course in this world. Therefore it is better for those with partial reason to follow the guidance of the saints.

In the fifth book of the Masnavi Rumi included several stories to illustrate why one should cut down the duck of gluttony, the cock of concupiscence, the peacock of ambition and ostentation, and the crow of bad desires. The story of how Muhammad converted a glutton who drank the milk of seven goats and then made a mess after being locked in a room shows the humility of the prophet in cleaning up the mess himself. He concluded that the infidels eat with seven bellies but the faithful with one.
The peacock catches people by displaying itself.

Pursuing the vulgar is like hunting a pig; the fatigue is extensive, and it is unlawful to eat it. Love alone is worth pursuing, but how can God be contained in anyone's trap? The most deadly evil eye is the eye of self-approval. The greed of the gluttonous duck is limited as is the greed of the lusty snake; but the peacock's ambition to rule can be many times as great.

Worldly wealth and even accomplishments can be enemies to the spiritual life. These are the human trials that create virtue. If there were no temptations, there could be no virtue.

Abraham killed the crow of desire in response to the command of God so that he would not crave anything else, and he killed the cock to subjugate pernicious desires.

Rumi suggested that God uses prophets and saints as mirrors to instruct people while the divine remains hidden behind the mirrors.

People hear the words from the mirrors but are ignorant that they are spoken by universal reason or the word of God. Ultimately God will place in people's hands their books of greed and generosity, of sin and piety, whatever they have practiced. When they awake on that morning, all the good and evil they have done will recur to them. After enumerating their faults, God in the end will grant them pardon as a free gift. To tell an angry person of faults, one must have a face as hard as a mirror to reflect the ugliness without fear or favor. Like 'Attar, Rumi wrote of the mystic's attaining annihilation, but he explained that the end and object of negation is to attain the subsequent affirmation just as the cardinal principle of Islam "There is no God" concludes with the affirmation "but God," and to the mystic this really means "There is nothing but God." Negation of the individual self clears the way for apprehending the existence of the One. The intoxication of life in pleasures and occupations which veil the truth should pass into the spiritual intoxication that lifts people to the beatific vision of eternal truth.

In the Discourses Rumi presented his teachings more directly. In the first chapter he suggested that the true scholar should serve God above the prince so that in their encounters the scholar will give more than take, thus making princes visitors of scholars rather than the reverse. Rumi advised stripping prejudices from one's discriminative faculty by seeing a friend in Faith, which is knowing who is one's true friend. Those who spend time with the undiscriminating have that faculty deteriorate and are unable to recognize a true friend in the Faith.

Rumi taught the universal principle that if you have done evil, you have done it to yourself, for how could wickedness reach out to affect God? Yet when you become straight, all your crookedness will disappear; so beware but have hope!
Those who assist an oppressor will find that God gives the oppressor power over them. God loves us by reproving us. One reproves friends, not a stranger. So long as you perceive longing and regret within yourself, that is proof that God loves and cares for you. If you perceive a fault in your brother, that fault is also within yourself.

The learned are like mirrors. Get rid of that fault in yourself, for
what distresses you about the other person distresses you inside
yourself. Rumi taught that all things in relation to God are good and
perfect, but in relation to humans some things are considered bad. To
a king prisons and gallows are part of the ornament of his kingdom;
but Rumi asked if to his people they are the same as robes of honor.
He argued that faith is better than prayer, because faith
without prayer is beneficial, but prayer without faith is not. Rumi
explained to his disciples that the desire to see the Master may
prevent them from perceiving the Master without a veil. He went on,
So it is with all desires and affections, all loves and fondnesses
which people have for every variety of thingfather,
mother, heaven, earth, gardens, palaces,
branches of knowledge, acts, things to eat and drink.

The man of God realizes that all these desires are the desire for God, and all those things are veils.

When men pass out of this world and behold that King without those veils, then they will realize that all these things were veils and coverings, their quest being in reality that One Thing.

All difficulties will then be resolved,

and they will hear in their hearts

the answer to all questions and all problems, and every thing will be seen face to face.

Rumi suggested God created these veils because if God's beauty were displayed without veils, we would not be able to endure and enjoy it just as the Sun lights up the world and warms us. The Sun enables trees and orchards to become fruitful, and its energy makes fruit that is unripe, bitter, and sour become mature

and sweet. Yet if the Sun came too near, it would not bestow benefits but destroy the whole world.

Rumi compared this world to the dream of a sleeper. It seems real while it is happening; but when one awakes, one does not benefit from the material things one had while asleep. The present then depends on what one requested while asleep.

God teaches in every way. A thief hanged on the gallows is an object lesson as is the person whom the king gives a robe of honor; but you should consider the difference between those two preachers. Even suffering is a divine grace, and hell becomes a place of worship as souls turn back to God just as being in prison or suffering pain often urges one to pray for relief. Yet after people are released or healed, they often forget to seek God. Believers, however, do not need to suffer, because even in ease they are mindful that suffering is constantly present. An intelligent child that has been punished does not forget the punishment; but the stupid child forgets it and is punished again. The wickedness and vice of humans can be great, because they are what veil the better element, which is also great. These veils cannot be removed without great striving, and Rumi recommended that the best method is to mingle with friends who have turned their backs to the world and their faces to God.

Moving Water When you do things from your soul, you feel a river
moving in you, a joy.
When actions come from another section, the feeling
disappears.
Don't let others lead you. They may be blind or, worse, vultures.
Reach for the rope of God. And what is that? Putting aside self-will.
Because of willfulness people sit in jail, the trapped bird's wings are
tied, fish sizzle in the skillet.
The anger of police is willfulness. You've seen a magistrate
inflict visible punishment.
Now see the invisible. If you could leave your selfishness, you
would see how you've been torturing your soul. We are born and live
inside black water in a well.
How could we know what an open field of sunlight is?
Don't insist on going where you think you want to go. Ask the way to
the spring.
Your living pieces will form a harmony.
There is a moving palace that floats in the air with balconies and clear
water flowing through, infinity everywhere, yet contained under a
single tent.

My Burning Heart

My heart is burning with love
All can see this flame
My heart is pulsing with passion
like waves on an ocean
my friends have become strangers
and I'm surrounded by enemies
But I'm free as the wind
no longer hurt by those who reproach me
I'm at home wherever I am
And in the room of lovers
I can see with closed eyes
the beauty that dances
Behind the veils
intoxicated with love
I too dance the rhythm
of this moving world
I have lost my senses
in my world of lovers

My Mother Was Fortune, My Father Generosity And Bounty

My mother was fortune, my father generosity and bounty; I
am joy, son of joy, son of joy, son of joy.
Behold, the Marquis of Glee has attainted felicity; this city and
plain are filled with soldiers and drums and flags.
If I encounter a wolf, he becomes moonfaced Joseph; if I go
down into a well, it converts into a Garden of Eram.
He whose heart is as iron and stone out of miserliness is now
changed before me into a Hatem of the age in generosity and
bounty.
Dust becomes gold and pure silver in my hand; how then
should the temptation of gold and silver waylay me?
I have an idol such that, were his sweet scent scattered
abroad, even an idol of stone would receive life through joy.
Sorrow has died for joy in him of "may God bind your consolation";
how should not such a sword strike the neck of sorrow?
By tyranny he seizes the soul of whom he desires; justices are
all slaves of such injustice and tyranny.
What is that mole on that face? Should it manifest itself, out
of desire for it forthwith maternal aunt would be estranged from
paternal [uncle].
I said, "If I am done and send my story, will you finish it and
expound it?" He answered, "Yes."

Not Here

There's courage involved if you want
to become truth.
There is a broken- open place in a lover.
Where are those qualities of bravery and
sharp compassion in this group? What's the
use of old and frozen thought?
I want a howling hurt. This is not a treasury
where gold is stored; this is for copper.
We alchemists look for talent that
can heat up and change.
Lukewarm won't do. Halfhearted holding back,
well-enough getting by? Not here.

Not Intrigued With Evening

What the material world values does
not shine the same in the truth of the soul.
You have been interested
in your shadow. Look instead directly at the sun.
What can we know by just
watching the time-and-space shapes of each other?
Someone half awake in the night sees imaginary dangers;
the morning star rises; the horizon grows
defined; people become friends in a moving caravan.
Night birds may think
daybreak a kind of darkness, because
that's all they know.
It's a fortunate
bird who's not intrigued with evening,
who flies in the sun we call Shams.

Nowruz

In my heart you are the mirthful ray
You are the caring, though my companions they
Happy is the world with the Nowruz and with the Eid
You are both my Eid and my Nowruz today

???? ?? ?? ??? ?? ????? ????
????? ????? ??? ????? ????
????? ??????? ?? ????? ? ?? ???
??? ?? ? ????? ?? ????? ????

O Love

O Love, O pure deep Love, be here, be now,
Be all - worlds dissolve into your
stainless endless radiance,
Frail living leaves burn with your brighter
than cold stares -
Make me your servant, your breath, your core.
O you who've gone on pilgrimage -
where are you, where, oh where?
Here, here is the Beloved!
Oh come now, come, oh come!
Your friend, he is your neighbor,
he is next to your wall -
You, erring in the desert -
what air of love is this?
If you'd see the Beloved's
form without any form -
You are the house, the master,
You are the Kaaba, you! . . .
Where is a bunch of roses,
if you would be this garden?
Where, one soul's pearly essence
when you're the Sea of God?
That's true - and yet your troubles
may turn to treasures rich -
How sad that you yourself veil
the treasure that is yours!

Ode 1373

I was dead, then alive.
Weeping, then laughing.
The power of love came into me,
and I became fierce like a lion,
then tender like the evening star.
He said, 'You're not mad enough.
You don't belong in this house.'
I went wild and had to be tied up.
He said, 'Still not wild enough
to stay with us!'
I broke through another layer
into joyfulness.
He said, 'Its not enough.'
I died.
He said, 'You are a clever little man,
full of fantasy and doubting.'
I plucked out my feathers and became a fool.
He said, 'Now you are the candle
for this assembly.'
But I'm no candle. Look!
I'm scattered smoke
He said, 'You are the Sheikh, the guide.'
But I'm not a teacher. I have no power.
He said, 'You already have wings.
I cannot give you wings.'
But I wanted his wings.
I felt like some flightless chicken.

Then new events said to me,
'Don't move. A sublime generosity is
coming towards you.'
And old love said, 'Stay with me.'

I said, 'I will.'
You are the fountain of the sun's light.
I am a willow shadow on the ground.
You make my raggedness silky.
The soul at dawn is like darkened water
that slowly begins to say Thank you, thank you.
Then at sunset, again, Venus gradually
Changes into the moon and then the whole nightsky.
This comes of smiling back
at your smile.
The chess master says nothing,
other than moving the silent chess piece.
That I am part of the ploys
of this game makes me
amazingly happy.

Ode 1620

There is a passion in me
that doesn't long for anything
from another human being.
I was given something else,
a cap to wear in both worlds.
It fell off. No matter.
One morning I went to a place beyond dawn.
A source of sweetness that flows
and is never less.
I have been shown a beauty
that would confuse both worlds,
but I won't cause that uproar.
I am nothing but a head
set on the ground
as a gift for Shams.

Ode 1823

I don't get tired of you. Don't grow weary
of being compassionate toward me!
All this thirst equipment
must surely be tired of me,
the waterjar, the water carrier.
I have a thirsty fish in me
that can never find enough
of what it's thirsty for!
Show me the way to the ocean!
Break these half-measures,
these small containers.
All this fantasy
and grief.
Let my house be drowned in the wave
that rose last night in the courtyard
hidden in the center of my chest.
Joseph fell like the moon into my well.
The harvest I expected was washed away.
But no matter.
A fire has risen above my tombstone hat.
I don't want learning, or dignity,
or respectability.
I want this music and this dawn
and the warmth of your cheek against mine.
The grief-armies assemble,
but I'm not going with them.
This is how it always is
when I finish a poem.
A great silence comes over me,
and I wonder why I ever thought
to use language.

Ode 1957: An Intellectual

An intellectual is all the time showing off.
Lovers dissolve and become bewildered.
Intellectuals try not to drown,
while the whole purpose of loves
is drowning.
Intellectual invent
ways to rest, and then lie down~
in those beds.
Lovers feel ashamed
of comforting ideas.
You've seen a glob
of oil on water? That's how a lover
sits with intellectuals, there, but alone
in a circle of himself.
Some intellectual
tries to give sound advice to a lover.
All he hears back is, I love you.
I love you.
Love is musk. Don't deny it
when you smell the scent!
Love is a tree.
Lovers, the shade of the long branches.
To the intellectual mind, a child must learn
to grow up and be adult.
In the station of love,
you see old men getting younger and younger.
Shams chose to live low in the roots
for you. So now, he soars in the air
as you sublimely articulating love!

Ode 2039

Go to your pillow and sleep, my son.
Leave me alone in the passion
Of this death-night.
Let the mill turn with your grieving.
But stay clear. Don't fall
into the river with me.
There's no way out,
no cure but death.
Last night in a dream I saw an old man
standing in a garden.
It was all Love.
He held out his hand and said,
Come toward me.
If there is a dragon on this path,
that old man has the emerald face
that can deflect it.
This is enough
I am leaving me self.
Bahauddin, my son,
if you want to be impressively learned,
memorize a famous historian,
and quote him as someone else!

Ode 2357

"Granite and Wineglass"
You are granite.
I am an empty wineglass.
You know what happens when we touch!
You laugh like the sun coming up laughs
at a star that disappears into it.
Love opens my chest, and thought
returns to its confines.
Patient and rational considerations leave.
Only passion stays, whimpering and feverish.
Some men fall down in the road like dregs thrown out.
Then, totally reckless, the next morning
they gallop out with new purposes. Love
is the reality, and poetry is the drum
that calls us to that. Don't keep complaining
about loneliness! Let the fear-language of that theme
crack open and float away. Let the priest come down
from his tower, and not go back up!

Ode 3079

We've come again to that knee of seacoast
no ocean can reach.
Tie together all human intellects.
They won't stretch to here.
The sky bares its neck so beautifully,
but gets no kiss. Only a taste.
This is the food that everyone wants,
wandering the wilderness, "Please give us
Your manna and quail."
We're here again with the Beloved.
This air, a shout. These meadowsounds,
an astonishing myth.
We've come into the Presence of the One
who was never apart from us.
When the waterbag is filling, you know
the Water-carrier's here!
The bag leans lovingly against Your shoulder.
"Without You I have no knowledge,
no way to touch anyone."
When someone chews sugarcane,
he's wanting this Sweetness.
Inside this globe the soul roars like thunder.
And now Silence, my strict tutor.
I won't try to talk about Shams.
Language cannot touch that Presence.

Ode 314

Those who don't feel this Love
pulling them like a river,
those who don't drink dawn
like a cup of spring water
or take in sunset like supper,
those who don't want to change,
let them sleep.
This Love is beyond the study of theology,
that old trickery and hypocrisy.
I you want to improve your mind that way,
sleep on.
I've given up on my brain.
I've torn the cloth to shreds
and thrown it away.
If you're not completely naked,
wrap your beautiful robe of words
around you, and sleep.

Ode 911

On the day I die, when I'm being
carried toward the grave, don't weep.
Don't say, 'He's gone! He's gone!'
Death has nothing to do with going away.
The sun sets and the moon sets,
but they're not gone. Death
is a coming together.
The tomb looks like a prison,
but it's really release
into Union.
The human seed goes down in the ground
like a bucket into the well where Joseph is.
It grows and comes up full
of some unimagined beauty.
Your mouth closes here
and immediately opens
with a shout of joy there.

One Swaying Being

Love is not condescension, never that, nor books, nor any marking on paper, nor what people say of each other. Love is a tree with branches reaching into eternity and roots set deep in eternity, and no trunk! Have you seen it? The mind cannot. Your desiring cannot. The longing you feel for this loves comes from inside you. When you become the Friend, your longing will be as the man in the ocean who holds to a piece of wood. Eventually, wood, man, and oceans become one swaying being,

One Whisper Of The Beloved

Lovers share a sacred decree –
to seek the Beloved.
They roll head over heels,
rushing toward the Beautiful One
like a torrent of water.
In truth, everyone is a shadow of the Beloved –
Our seeking is His seeking,
Our words are His words.
At times we flow toward the Beloved
like a dancing stream.
At times we are still water
held in His pitcher.
At times we boil in a pot
turning to vapor –
that is the job of the Beloved.
He breathes into my ear
until my soul
takes on His fragrance.
He is the soul of my soul –
How can I escape?
But why would any soul in this world
want to escape from the Beloved?
He will melt your pride
making you thin as a strand of hair,
Yet do not trade, even for both worlds,
One strand of His hair.
We search for Him here and there
while looking right at Him.
Sitting by His side we ask,
'O Beloved, where is the Beloved?'
Enough with such questions! –
Let silence take you to the core of life.
All your talk is worthless
When compared to one whisper of the Beloved.

Only Breath

Not Christian or Jew or Muslim, not Hindu
Buddhist, sufi, or zen. Not any religion
or cultural system. I am not from the East
or the West, not out of the ocean or up
from the ground, not natural or ethereal, not
composed of elements at all. I do not exist,
am not an entity in this world or in the next,
did not descend from Adam and Eve or any
origin story. My place is placeless, a trace
of the traceless. Neither body or soul.
I belong to the beloved, have seen the two
worlds as one and that one call to and know,
first, last, outer, inner, only that
breath breathing human being.

Our Death Is Our Wedding With Eternity

Our death is our wedding with eternity.
What is the secret? 'God is One.'
The sunlight splits when entering the windows of the house.
This multiplicity exists in the cluster of grapes;
It is not in the juice made from the grapes.
For he who is living in the Light of God,
The death of the carnal soul is a blessing.
Regarding him, say neither bad nor good,
For he is gone beyond the good and the bad.
Fix your eyes on God and do not talk about what is invisible,
So that he may place another look in your eyes.
It is in the vision of the physical eyes
That no invisible or secret thing exists.
But when the eye is turned toward the Light of God
What thing could remain hidden under such a Light?
Although all lights emanate from the Divine Light
Don't call all these lights 'the Light of God';
It is the eternal light which is the Light of God,
The ephemeral light is an attribute of the body and the flesh.
...Oh God who gives the grace of vision!
The bird of vision is flying towards You with the wings of desire.

Out Beyond Ideas

Out beyond ideas of wrongdoing and rightdoing,
there is a field. I'll meet you there.
When the soul lies down in that grass,
the world is too full to talk about.
Ideas, language, even the phrase each other
doesn't make any sense

Out Of Your Love

Out of your love the fire of youth will rise.
In the chest, visions of the soul will rise.
If you are going to kill me, kill me, it is alright.
When the friend kills, a new life will rise.

Passion Makes The Old Medicine New:

Passion makes the old medicine new:
Passion lops off the bough of weariness.
Passion is the elixir that renews:
how can there be weariness
when passion is present?
Oh, don't sigh heavily from fatigue:
seek passion, seek passion, seek passion!

Quatrain 1693 (Farsi With English Translation)

ay sâqî, az-ân bâda ke awwal dâd-î
riTlê dô dar andâz-o be-y-afzâ shâdî
yâ châshniyê az-ân na-bâyast namûd
yâ mast-o kharâb kon, chô sar be-g'shâd-î

English Translation
O cupbearer, from that wine which you first gave,
Toss in two [more] cups worth and increase (my) happiness.
Either a taste of it must not be made known,
Or, if you have opened the [jug's] top, you must make (me)drunk and
ruined.

Reason Says Love Says

Reason says, " I will beguile him with the tongue."; Love says,
"Be silent. I will beguile him with the soul."
The soul says to the heart, "Go, do not laugh at me and yourself.
What is there that is not his, that I may beguile him
thereby?"
He is not sorrowful and anxious and seeking oblivion that I
may beguile him with wine and a heavy measure.
The arrow of his glance needs not a bow that I should beguile
the shaft of his gaze with a bow.
He is not prisoner of the world, fettered to this world of earth,
that I should beguile him with gold of the kingdom of the world.
He is an angel, though in form he is a man; he is not lustful
that I should beguile him with women.
Angels start away from the house wherein this form is, so how
should I beguile him with such a form and likeness?
He does not take a flock of horses, since he flies on wings; his
food is light, so how should I beguile him with bread?
He is not a merchant and trafficker in the market of the world
that I should beguile him with enchantment of grain and loss.
He is not veiled that I should make myself out sick and utter
sighs, to beguile him with lamentation.

I will bind my head and bow my head, for I have got out of
hand; I will not beguile his compassion with sickness or fluttering.
Hair by hair he sees my crookedness and feigning; what's
hidden from him that I should beguile him with anything hidden.
He is not a seeker of fame, a prince addicted to poets, that I
should beguile him with verses and lyrics and flowing poetry.
The glory of the unseen form is too great for me to beguile it
with blessing or Paradise.
Shams-e Tabriz, who is his chosen and beloved–perchance I
will beguile him with this same pole of the age.

Rise, lovers, that we may go towards heaven; we have seen this world,
so let us go to that world.
No, no, for thought these two gardens are beautiful and fair, let us
pass beyond these two, and go to that Gardener.
Let us go prostrating to the sea like a torrent, then let us go foaming
upon the face of the sea.
Let us journey from this street of mourning to the wedding feast, let
us go from this saffron face to the face of the Judas tree blossom.
Trembling like a leaf and twig from fear of falling, our hearts are
throbbing; let us go to the Abode of Security.
There is no escape from pain, since we are in exile, and there is no
escape from dust, seeing that we are going to a dustbowl.
Like parrots green of wing and with fine pinions, let us become
sugar-gatherers and go to the sugar-bed.
These forms are signs of the signless fashioner; hidden from the evil
eye, come, let us go to the signless.
It is a road full of tribulation, but love is the guide, giving us
instruction how we should go thereon;
Though the shadow of the king's grace surely protects, yet it is better
that on that road we go with the caravan.
We are like rain falling on a leaky roof; let us spring from the leak and
go by that waterspout.

We are crooked as a bow, for the string is in our own throats; when we become straight, then we will go like an arrow from the bow.
We cower like mice in the house because of the cats; if we are lion's whelps, let us go to that Lion.
Let us make our soul a mirror in passion for a Joseph; let us go before Joseph's beauty with a present.
Let us be silent, that the giver of speech may say this; even as he shall say, so let us go. F 1713
"Street of Mourning": The world, which has been called by many similar names,
such as "the infidel's paradise," and symbolized by the false dawn, a carcass, a
bath-stove and a tomb. (Cf. "World" in Nicholson's index to Math .).

Shadow And Light Source Both

How does a part of the world leave the world?
How does wetness leave water?
Dont' try to put out fire by throwing on
more fire! Don't wash a wound with blood.
No matter how fast you run, your shadow
keeps up. Sometimes it's in front!
Only full overhead sun diminishes your shadow.
But that shadow has been serving you.
What hurts you, blesses you. Darkness is
your candle. Your boundaries are your quest.
I could explain this, but it will break the
glass cover on your heart, and there's no fixing that.
You must have shadow and light source both.
Listen, and lay your head under the tree of awe.
When from that tree feathers and wings sprout on you,
be quieter than a dove. Don't even open your mouth for even a coo.

Sleep Of The Body The Soul's Awakening

Every night Thou freest our spirits from the body
And its snare, making them pure as rased tablets.
Every night spirits are released from this cage,
And set free, neither lording it nor lorded over.
At night prisoners are unaware of their prison,
At night kings are unaware of their majesty.
Then there is no thought or care for loss or gain,
No regard to such an one or such an one.
The state of the 'Knower' is such as this, even when awake.
God says,4 'Thou wouldst deem him awake though asleep,
Sleeping to the affairs of the world, day and night,
Like a pen in the directing hand of the writer.
He who sees not the hand which effects the writing
Fancies the effect proceeds from the motion of the pen.
If the 'Knower' revealed the particulars of this state,
'Twould rob the vulgar of their sensual sleep.
His soul wanders in the desert that has no similitude;
Like his body, his spirit is enjoying perfect rest;
Freed from desire of eating and drinking,
Like a bird escaped from cage and snare.
But when he is again beguiled into the snare,
He cries for help to the Almighty.

Soul Receives From Soul

Soul receives from soul that knowledge,
therefore not by book nor from tongue.
If knowledge of mysteries come after
emptiness of mind, that is illumination of heart.

That Lives In Us

If you put your hands on this oar with me,
they will never harm another, and they will come to find
they hold everything you want.
If you put your hands on this oar with me, they would no longer
lift anything to your
mouth that might wound your precious landthat
sacred earth that is
your body.
If you put your soul against this oar with me,
the power that made the universe will enter your sinew
from a source not outside your limbs, but from a holy realm
that lives in us.
Exuberant is existence, time a husk.
When the moment cracks open, ecstasy leaps out and devours space;
love goes mad with the blessings, like my words give.
Why lay yourself on the torturer's rack of the past and future?
The mind that tries to shape tomorrow beyond its capacities
will find no rest.
Be kind to yourself, dear- to our innocent follies.
Forget any sounds or touch you knew that did not help you dance.
You will come to see that all evolves us.
If you put your heart against the earth with me, in serving
every creature, our Beloved will enter you from our sacred realm
and we will be, we will be
so happy.

The Agony And Ecstasy

In the orchard and rose garden
I long to see your face.
In the taste of Sweetness
I long to kiss your lips.
In the shadows of passion
I long for your love.
Oh! Supreme Lover!
Let me leave aside my worries.
The flowers are blooming
with the exultation of your Spirit.
By Allah!
I long to escape the prison of my ego
and lose myself
in the mountains and the desert.
These sad and lonely people tire me.
I long to revel in the drunken frenzy of your love
and feel the strength of Rustam in my hands.
I'm sick of mortal kings.
I long to see your light.
With lamps in hand
the sheiks and mullahs roam
the dark alleys of these towns
not finding what they seek.
You are the Essence of the Essence,
The intoxication of Love.
I long to sing your praises
but stand mute
with the agony of wishing in my heart.

The Beauty Of The Heart

The beauty of the heart
is the lasting beauty:
its lips give to drink
of the water of life.
Truly it is the water,
that which pours,
and the one who drinks.
All three become one when
your talisman is shattered.
That oneness you can't know
by reasoning.

The breeze at dawn has secrets to tell you.
Don't go back to sleep.
You must ask for what you really want.
Don't go back to sleep.
People are going back and forth across the doorsill
where the two worlds touch.
The door is round and open.
Don't go back to sleep.

The Chance Of Humming

A man
standing on two logs in a river
might do all right floating with the current
while humming in the now.
Though if one log is tied to a camel,
who is also heading south along the bank - at the same paceall
could still be well with the world unless the camel
thinks he forgot something, and abruptly turns upstream,
then uh-oh.
Most minds do not live in the present
and can stick to a reasonable plan; most minds abruptly turn
and undermine the chance of humming.

The Guest House

This being human is a guest house.
Every morning a new arrival.
A joy, a depression, a meanness,
some momentary awareness comes
As an unexpected visitor.
Welcome and entertain them all!
Even if they're a crowd of sorrows,
who violently sweep your house
empty of its furniture,
still treat each guest honorably.
He may be clearing you out
for some new delight.
The dark thought, the shame, the malice,
meet them at the door laughing,
and invite them in.
Be grateful for whoever comes,
because each has been sent
as a guide from beyond.

The Lovers

The Lovers
will drink wine night and day.
They will drink until they can
tear away the veils of intellect and
melt away the layers of shame and modesty.
When in Love,
body, mind, heart and soul don't even exist.
Become this,
fall in Love, and you will not be separated again.

The Meaning Of Love

Both light and shadow
are the dance of Love.
Love has no cause;
it is the astrolabe of God's secrets.
Lover and Loving are inseparable
and timeless.
Although I may try to describe Love
when I experience it I am speechless.
Although I may try to write about Love
I am rendered helpless;
my pen breaks and the paper slips away
at the ineffable place
where Lover, Loving and Loved are one.
Every moment is made glorious
by the light of Love.

The Privileged Lovers

The moon has become a dancer
at this festival of love.
This dance of light,
This sacred blessing,
This divine love,
beckons us
to a world beyond
only lovers can see
with their eyes of fiery passion.
They are the chosen ones
who have surrendered.
Once they were particles of light
now they are the radiant sun.
They have left behind
the world of deceitful games.
They are the privileged lovers
who create a new world
with their eyes of fiery passion.
Translated by: Fereydoun Kia

The Ravings Which My Enemy Uttered I Heard Within

My Heart

The ravings which my enemy uttered I heard within my heart;
the secret thoughts he harbored against me I also perceived.
His dog bit my foot, he showed me much injustice; I do not
bite him like a dog, I have bitten my own lip.
Since I have penetrated into the secrets of individuals like men
of God, why should I take glory in having penetrated his secret?
I reproach myself that through my doubtings it so happened
that purposely I drew a scorpion towards my own foot.
Like Eblis who saw nothing of Adam except his fire, by God I
was invisible to his insignificant Eblis.
Convey to my friends why I am afflicted in mind; when the
snake bit my thigh I started away from the black rope.
The blessed silent ones, their lips and eyes closed -by a way
unknown to any man, I ran into their thoughts;
Since there is a secret and perfect way from heart to heart, I
gathered gold and silver from the treasuries of hearts.
Into the thought that was like a brazen stove I flung the dead
dog; out of the thought that was like a rose bower I plucked roses
and jasmine.
If I have hinted at the evil and good ofm y friends,
I have spun flax like a weaver as the choicest veil.

When my heart rushed suddenly to a heart mighty and aware,
out of awe for his heart I fluttered like the heart.
As you are happy with your own state, how did you fall in with
me? Attend to your own business, for I am neither shaikh nor
disciple.
As far as you are concerned, brother, I am neither copper nor
red gold; drive me from your door, for I am neither lock nor key.
Take it as if I had not ever spoken these words; if you had been
in my mind, by God I would not have quarreled.

The Rubaiyat Of Rumi

Time bringeth swift to end
The rout men keep;
Death's wolf is nigh to rend
These silly sheep.
See, how in pride they go
With lifted head,
Till Fate with a sudden blow
Smiteth them dead.

2.

Thou who lovest, life a crow,
Winter's chill and winter's snow,
Ever exiled from the vale's
Roses red, and nightingales:
Take this moment to thy heart!
When the moment shall depart,
Long thou 'lt seek it as it flies
With a hundred lamps and eyes.

3.

The heavenly rider passed;
The dust rose in the air;
He sped; but the dust he cast
Yet hangeth there.
Straight forward thy vision be,
And gaze not left or night;
His dust is here, and he
In the Infinite.

4.

Who was he that said
The immortal spirit is dead,
Or how dared he say
Hope's sun hath passed away?
An enemy of the sun,

Standing his roof upon,
Bound up both his eyes
And cried: 'Lo, the sun dies!'

5.
'Who lifteth up the spirit,
Say, who is he?'
'Who gave in the beginning
This life to me.
Who hoodeth, life a falcon's,
Awhile mine eyes,
But presently shall loose me
To hunt my prize.'
6.
As salt resolved in the ocean
I was swallowed in God's sea,
Past faith, past unbelieving,
Past doubt, past certainty.
Suddenly in my bosom
A star shone clear and bright;
All the suns of heaven
Vanished in that star's light.
~

Flowers every night
Blossom in the sky;
Peace in the Infinite;
At peace am I.
Sighs a hundredfold
From my heart arise;
My heart, dark and cold,
Flames with my sighs.
7.
He that is my souls' repose
Round my heart encircling goes,
Round my heart and soul of bliss
He encircling is.
Laughing from my earthy bed

Like a tree I lift my head,
For the Fount of Living mirth
Washes round my earth.
8.
The breeze of the morn

Scatters musk in its train,
Fragrance borne
From my fair love's lane.
Ere the world wastes,
Sleep no more: arise!
The caravan hastes,
The sweet scent dies.
9.
If life be gone, fresh life to you
God offereth,
A life eternal to renew
This life of death.
The Fount of Immorality
In Love is found;
The come, and in this boundless sea
Of Love be drowned.
10.
Happy was I
In the pearl's heart to lie;
Till, lashed by life's hurricane,
Life a tossed wave I ran.
The secret of the sea
I uttered thunderously;
Like a spent cloud on the shore
I slept, and stirred no more.
11.
He set the world aflame,
And laid me on the same;
A hundred tongues of fire
Lapped round my pyre.
And when the blazing tide

Engulfed me, and I sighed,
Upon my mouth in haste
His hand He placed.
12.
Though every way I try
His whim to satisfy,
His every answering word

Is a pointed sword.
See how the blood drips
From His finger-tips;
Why does He find it good
To wash in my blood?
13.
Remembering Thy lip,
The ruby red I kiss;
Having not that to sip,
My lips press this.
Not to Thy far sky
Reaches my stretched hand,
Wherefore kneeling, I
Embrace the land.
14.
I sought a soul in the sea
And found a coral there;
Beneath the foam for me
An ocean was all laid bare.
Into my heart's night
Along a narrow way
I groped; and lo! the light,
An infinite land of day.

The Seed Market

Can you find another market like this?
Where, with your one rose
you can buy hundreds of rose gardens?
Where, for one seed get a whole wilderness?
For one weak breath, a divine wind?
You've been fearful
of being absorbed in the ground,
or drawn up by the air.
Now, your waterbead lets go
and drops into the ocean, where it came from.
It no longer has the form it had,
but it's still water
The essence is the same.
This giving up is not a repenting.
It's a deep honoring of yourself.
When the ocean comes to you as a lover,
marry at once, quickly, for God's sake!
Don't postpone it!
Existence has no better gift.
No amount of searching will find this.
A perfect falcon, for no reason
has landed on your shoulder,
and become yours.

The Self We Share

Thirst is angry with water. Hunger bitter
with bread.
The cave wants nothing to do with the sun.
This is dumb, the self- defeating way
we've been.
A gold mine is calling us into its temple.
Instead, we bend and keep picking up rocks
from the ground.
Every thing has a shine like gold,
but we should turn to the source!
The origin is what we truly are. I add a little
vinegar to the honey I give.
The bite of scolding makes ecstasy more familiar.
But look, fish, you're already in the ocean:
just swimming there makes you friends with
glory.
What are these grudges about? You are Benjamin.
Joseph has put a gold cup in your grain sack and
accused you of being a thief.
Now he draws you aside and says,
'You are my brother. I
am a prayer. You're the amen.'
We move in eternal regions, yet
worry about property here.
This is the prayer of each:
You are the source of my life.

You separate essence from mud.
You honor my soul. You bring rivers
from themountain springs. You brighten my eyes.
The wine you offer takes me out of myself into
the self we share. Doing that is religion.

The Springtime Of Lovers Has Come

The springtime of Lovers has come,
that this dust bowl may become a garden;
the proclamation of heaven has come,
that the bird of the soul may rise in flight.
The sea becomes full of pearls,
the salt marsh becomes sweet as kauthar,
the stone becomes a ruby from the mine,
the body becomes wholly soul.

The Taste Of Morning

Time's knife slides from the sheath,
as fish from where it swims.
Being closer and closer is the desire
of the body. Don't wish for union!
There's a closeness beyond that. Why
would God want a second God? Fall in
love in such a way that it frees you
from any connecting. Love is the soul's
light, the taste of morning, no me, no
we, no claim of being. These words
are the smoke the fire gives off as it
absolves its defects, as eyes in silence,
tears, face. Love cannot be said.

The Temple Of Love

The temple of love is not love itself;
True love is the treasure,
Not the walls about it.
Do not admire the decoration,
But involve yourself in the essence,
The perfume that invades and touches you-
The beginning and the end.
Discovered, this replace all else,
The apparent and the unknowable.
Time and space are slaves to this presence.

The Time Has Come For Us To Become Madmen In

Your Chain
The time has come for us to become madmen in your chain, to burst our bonds and become estranged from all;
To yield up our souls, no more to bear the disgrace of such a soul, to set fire to our house, and run like fire to the tavern.
Until we ferment, we shall not escape from this vat of the world- how then shall we become intimate with the lip of that flagon and bowl?
Listen to the words from a madman: do not suppose that we become true men until we die.
It is necessary that we should become more inverted than the tip of a comb in the top of the twisted tress of felicity;
Spread our wings and pinions like a tree in the orchard, if like a seed we are to be scattered on this road of annihilation.
Though we are of stone, we shall become like wax for you seal; though we be candles, we shall become a moth in the track of your light.
Though we are kings, we shall travel straight as rocks for your sake, that we may become blessed through your queen on this chessboard.

In the face of the mirror of love we must not breathe a word of
ourselves; we must become intimate with your treasure when
we are changed to waste.
Like the tale of the heart we must be without bread or ending,
that we may become dwellers in the heart of lovers like a tale.
If he acts like the seeker, we shall attain to being sought; if he acts
the key, we shall become all the wards of the lock.
If Mostafa does not make his way and couch in our hearts, it is
meet that we should lament and become like the Wailing
Column.
No, be silent; for one must observe silence towards the watchman
when we go towards the pavilion by night.

The Way Things Should

What will
our children do in the morning?
Will they wake with their hearts wanting to play,
the way wings
should?
Will they have dreamed the needed flights and gathered
the strength from the planets that all
men and women need to balance
the wonderful charms of
the earth
so that her power and beauty does not make us forget our own?
I know all about the ways of the heart - how it wants to be alive.
Love so needs to love
that it will endure almost anything, even abuse,
just to flicker for a moment. But the sky's mouth is kind,
its song will never hurt you, for I sing those words.
What will our children do in the morning
if they do not see us
fly?

There Are A Hundred Kinds Of Prayer (Quatrain In

Farsi With English Translation)
emrôz chô har rôz, kharâb-êm kharâb
ma-g'shâ dar andêsha-wo bar gîr rabâb
Sad gôna namâz-ast-o rukû`-ast-o sujûd
ân-râ ke jamâl-é dôst bâsh-ad miHrâb

Today, like every day, we are ruined, ruined (by 'wine').
Don't open the door of worry, but take up the lute!
There are a hundred kinds of prayer, bowing, and prostration6
For the one whose prayer-niche, is the beauty of the Beloved

There Is A Candle In Your Heart

There is a candle in the heart of man, waiting to be kindled.
In separation from the Friend, there is a cut waiting to be stitched.
O, you who are ignorant of endurance and the burning fire of love--
Love comes of its own free will, it can't be learned in any school.

There Is A Community Of Spirit

There is a community of the spirit.
Join it, and feel the delight
of walking in the noisy street
and being the noise.
Drink all your passion,
and be a disgrace.
Close both eyes
to see with the other eye.

There Is A Life-Force Within Your Soul

There is a life-force within your soul, seek that life.
There is a gem in the mountain of your body, seek that
mine.
O traveler, if you are in search of That
Don't look outside, look inside yourself and seek That.

There Is A Way

There is a way between voice and presence
where information flows.
In disciplined silence it opens.
With wandering talk it closes.

This Aloneness

This aloneness is worth more than a thousand lives.
This freedom is worth more than all the lands on earth.
To be one with the truth for just a moment,
Is worth more than the world and life itself.

This Is Love

This is love: to fly toward a secret sky,
to cause a hundred veils to fall each moment.
First, to let go of live.
In the end, to take a step without feet;
to regard this world as invisible,
and to disregard what appears to be the self.
Heart, I said, what a gift it has been
to enter this circle of lovers,
to see beyond seeing itself,
to reach and feel within the breast.

This Is Love

This is love: to fly to heaven, every moment to rend a hundred veils;
At first instance, to break away from breath -
first step, to renounce feet;
To disregard this world, to see only that which you yourself have seen
I said,
'Heart, congratulations on entering the circle of lovers,
'On gazing beyond the range of the eye,
on running into the alley of the breasts.'
Whence came this breath, O heart?
Whence came this throbbing, O heart?
Bird, speak the tongue of birds: I can heed your cipher!
The heart said, 'I was in the factory whilst the home of water and clay was
abaking.
'I was flying from the workshop whilst the workshop was being created.
'When I could no more resist, they dragged me; how shall I
tell the manner of that dragging? '

This We Have Now

This we have now
is not imagination.
This is not
grief or joy.
Not a judging state,
or an elation,
or sadness.
Those come and go.
This is the presence that doesn't.

This Will Not Win Him

Reason says,
I will win him with my eloquence.
Love says,
I will win him with my silence.
Soul says,
How can I ever win him
When all I have is already his?
He does not want, he does not worry,
He does not seek a sublime state of euphoria -
How then can I win him
With sweet wine or gold?
He is not bound by the senses -
How then can I win him
With all the riches of China?
He is an angel,
Though he appears in the form of a man.
Even angels cannot fly in his presence -
How then can I win him
By assuming a heavenly form?
He flies on the wings of God,
His food is pure light -
How then can I win him
With a loaf of baked bread?
He is neither a merchant, nor a tradesman -
How then can I win him
With a plan of great profit?
He is not blind, nor easily fooled -
How then can I win him
By lying in bed as if gravely ill?
I will go mad, pull out my hair,

Grind my face in the dirt -
How will this win him?

He sees everything -
how can I ever fool him?
He is not a seeker of fame,
A prince addicted to the praise of poets -
How then can I win him
With flowing rhymes and poetic verses?
The glory of his unseen form
Fills the whole universe
How then can I win him
With a mere promise of paradise?
I may cover the earth with roses,
I may fill the ocean with tears,
I may shake the heavens with praises -
none of this will win him.
There is only one way to win him,
this Beloved of mine -
Become his.

Two Friends

A certain person came to the Friend's door
and knocked.
'Who's there?'
'It's me.'
The Friend answered, 'Go away. There's no place
for raw meat at this table.'
The individual went wandering for a year.
Nothing but the fire of separation
can change hypocrisy and ego. The person returned
completely cooked,
walked up and down in front of the Friend's house,
gently knocked.
'Who is it?'
'You.'
'Please come in, my self,
there's no place in this house for two.
The doubled end of the thread is not what goes through
the eye of the needle.
It's a single-pointed, fined-down, thread end,
not a big ego-beast with baggage.'

Two Kinds Of Intelligence
There are two kinds of intelligence: one acquired,
as a child in school memorizes facts and concepts
from books and from what the teacher says,
collecting information from the traditional sciences
as well as from the new sciences.
With such intelligence you rise in the world.
You get ranked ahead or behind others
in regard to your competence in retaining
information. You stroll with this intelligence
in and out of fields of knowledge, getting always more
marks on your preserving tablets.

There is another kind of tablet, one
already completed and preserved inside you.
A spring overflowing its springbox. A freshness
in the center of the chest. This other intelligence
does not turn yellow or stagnate. It's fluid,
and it doesn't move from outside to inside
through conduits of plumbing-learning.
This second knowing is a fountainhead
from within you, moving out.

Until You've Found Pain

Until you've found pain, you won't reach the cure
Until you've given up life, you won't unite with
the supreme soul
Until you've found fire inside yourself, like the Friend,
You won't reach the spring of life, like Khezr.

Untitled
The minute I heard my first love story
I started looking for you, not knowing
how blind that was.
Lovers don't finally meet somewhere
They're in each other all along.

We Are As The Flute

We are as the flute, and the music in us is from thee;
we are as the mountain and the echo in us is from thee.
We are as pieces of chess engaged in victory and defeat:
our victory and defeat is from thee,
O thou whose qualities are comely!
Who are we, O Thou soul of our souls,
that we should remain in being beside thee?
We and our existences are really non-existence;
thou art the absolute Being which manifests the perishable.
We all are lions, but lions on a banner:
because of the wind they are rushing
onward from moment to moment.
Their onward rush is visible,
and the wind is unseen:
may that which is unseen not fail from us!
Our wind whereby we are moved and our being are of thy gift;
our whole existence is from thy bringing into being.

Weary Not Of Us, For We Are Very Beautiful

Weary not of us, for we are very beautiful; it is out of very jealousy and proper pride that we entered the veil.
On the day when we cast of the body's veil from the soul, you will see that we are the envy of despair of man and the Polestars.
Wash your face and become clean for beholding us, else remain afar, for we are beloveds of ourselves.
We are not that beauty who tomorrow will become a crone; till eternity we are young and heart-comforting and fair of stature.
If that veil become worn out, the beauty has not grown old; the life of the Veil is transient, and we are boundless life.
When Eblis saw the veil of Adam, he refused; Adam called to him, "You are the rejected one, not I."
The rest of the angels fell down prostrate, saying as they bowed themselves, "We have encountered a beauty:
"Beneath the veil is an idol who by his qualities robbed us of reason, and we, prostrate, fell."
If our reason does not know the forms of the foul old men from those of the beauties, we are apostates from love.
What place is there for a beauty? For he is the Lion of God. Like a child we prattled, for we are children of the alphabet.
Children are beguiled with nuts and raisins, else, how are we meet for nuts and sesame-grains?
When an old woman is hidden in helmet and chainmail, she says, "I am the illustrious Rostam of the battle ranks."
By her boast all know that she is a woman; how should we make a mistake, seeing that we are in the light of Ahmad?

"The believer is discriminating" - so said the Prophet; now close your
mouth, for we are guided rightly without speech.
Hear the rest of from Shams the Pride of Tabiz for we did not take
the end of the story from that king.

What Hidden Sweetness Is There

What hidden sweetness there is in this emptiness of the belly!
Man is surely like a lute, no more and no less;
For if, for instance, the belly of the lute becomes full, no
lament high or low will arise from that full lute.
If your brain and belly are on fire through fasting, because of
the fire every moment a lament will arise from your breast.
Every moment you will burn a thousand veils by that fire; you
will mount a hundred steps with zeal and endeavor.
Become empty of belly, and weep entreatingly like the reed
pipe; become empty of belly, and tell secrets with the reed pen.
If your belly is full at the time of concourse, it will bring Satan
in place of your reason, an idol in place of the Kaaba.
When you keep the fast, good habits gather together before
you like slaves and servants and retinue.
Keep the fast, for that is Solomon's ring; give not the ring to
the div, destroy not your kingdom.
Even if your kingdom has gone from your head and your army
has fled, your army will rise up, pennants flying above them.
The table arrived from heaven to the tents of the fast,
 by the intervention of the prayers of Jesus, son of Mary.
In the fast, be expectant of the table of
bounty, for the table of
bounty is better than the broth of cabbages.

What Was Told, That

What was said to the rose that made it open was said
to me here in my chest.
What was told the cypress that made it strong
and straight, what was
whispered the jasmine so it is what it is, whatever made
sugarcane sweet, whatever
was said to the inhabitants of the town of Chigil in
Turkestan that makes them
so handsome, whatever lets the pomegranate flower blush
like a human face, that is
being said to me now. I blush. Whatever put eloquence in
language, that's happening here.
The great warehouse doors open; I fill with gratitude,
chewing a piece of sugarcane,
in love with the one to whom every that belongs!

When Grapes Turn To Wine

When grapes turn
to wine, they long for our ability to change.
When stars wheel
around the North Pole,
they are longing for our growing consciousness.
Wine got drunk with us,
not the other way.
The body developed out of us, not we from it.
We are bees,
and our body is a honeycomb.
We made
the body, cell by cell we made it.
translated by Robert Bly

When I Am Asleep And Crumbling In The Tomb

When I am asleep and crumbling in the tomb, should you come
to visit me, I will come forth with speed.
You are for me the blast of the trumpet and the resurrection,
so what shall I do? Dead or living, wherever you are, there am I.
Without your lip I am a frozen and silent reed; what melodies
I play the moment you breathe on my reed!
Your wretched reed has become accustomed to your sugar lip;
remember wretched me, for I am seeking you.
When I do not find the moon of your countenance, I bind up
my head [veil myself in your mourning]; when I do not find your
sweet lip, gnaw my own hand.

When I Die

When I die
when my coffin
is being taken out
you must never think
i am missing this world
don't shed any tears
don't lament or
feel sorry
i'm not falling
into a monster's abyss
when you see
my corpse is being carried
don't cry for my leaving
i'm not leaving
i'm arriving at eternal love
when you leave me
in the grave
don't say goodbye
remember a grave is
only a curtain
for the paradise behind
you'll only see me
descending into a grave
now watch me rise
how can there be an end
when the sun sets or
the moon goes down
it looks like the end
it seems like a sunset
but in reality it is a dawn
when the grave locks you up
that is when your soul is freed
have you ever seen

a seed fallen to earth
not rise with a new life
why should you doubt the rise
of a seed named human
have you ever seen
a bucket lowered into a well
coming back empty
why lament for a soul
when it can come back
like Joseph from the well
when for the last time
you close your mouth
your words and soul
will belong to the world of
no place no time

When The Rose Is Gone

When the rose is gone and the garden faded
you will no longer hear the nightingale's song.
The Beloved is all; the lover just a veil.
The Beloved is living; the lover a dead thing.
If love withholds its strengthening care,
the lover is left like a bird without care,
the lover is left like a bird without wings.
How will I be awake and aware
if the light of the Beloved is absent?
Love wills that this Word be brought forth

Who Is At My Door?

He said, 'Who is at my door?'
I said, 'Your humble servant.'
He said, 'What business do you have?'
I said, 'To greet you, 0 Lord.'
He said, 'How long will you journey on?'
I said, 'Until you stop me.'
He said, 'How long will you boil in the fire?'
I said, 'Until I am pure.

'This is my oath of love.
For the sake of love
I gave up wealth and position.'
He said, 'You have pleaded your case
but you have no witness.'
I said, 'My tears are my witness;
the pallor of my face is my proof.'
He said, 'Your witness has no credibility;
your eyes are too wet to see.'
I said, 'By the splendor of your justice
my eyes are clear and faultless.'
He said, 'What do you seek?'
I said, 'To have you as my constant friend.'
He said, 'What do you want from me?'
I said, 'Your abundant grace.'
He said, 'Who was your companion on the journey?
I said, 'The thought of you, 0 King.'
He said, 'What called you here?'
I said, 'The fragrance of your wine.'
He said, 'What brings you the most fulfillment?'
I said, 'The company of the Emperor.'
He said, 'What do you find there?'
I said, 'A hundred miracles.'
He said, 'Why is the palace deserted?'
I said, 'They all fear the thief.'

He said, 'Who is the thief?'
I said, 'The one who keeps me from -you.
He said, 'Where is there safety?'
I said, 'In service and renunciation.'
He said, 'What is there to renounce?'
I said, 'The hope of salvation.'
He said, 'Where is there calamity?'
I said, 'In the presence of your love.'
He said, 'How do you benefit from this life?'
I said, 'By keeping true to myself
Now it is time for silence.
If I told you about His true essence
You would fly from your self and be gone,
and neither door nor roof could hold you back!

Who Makes These Changes?

Who makes these changes?
I shoot an arrow right.
It lands left.
I ride after a deer and find myself
Chased by a hog.
I plot to get what I want
And end up in prison.
I dig pits to trap others
And fall in.
I should be suspicious
Of what I want.

Who Says Words With My Mouth?

All day I think about it, then at night I say it.
Where did I come from, and what am I supposed to be doing?
I have no idea.
My soul is from elsewhere, I'm sure of that,
and I intend to end up there.
This drunkenness began in some other tavern.
When I get back around to that place,
I'll be completely sober. Meanwhile,
I'm like a bird from another continent, sitting in this aviary.
The day is coming when I fly off,
but who is it now in my ear who hears my voice?
Who says words with my mouth?
Who looks out with my eyes? What is the soul?
I cannot stop asking.
If I could taste one sip of an answer,
I could break out of this prison for drunks.
I didn't come here of my own accord, and I can't leave that way.
Whoever brought me here will have to take me home.
This poetry, I never know what I'm going to say.
I don't plan it.
When I'm outside the saying of it,
I get very quiet and rarely speak at all.

Whoever Brought Me Here

All day I think about it, then at night I say it.
Where did I come from, and what am I supposed to be doing?
I have no idea.
My soul is from elsewhere, I'm sure of that,
and I intend to end up there.
This drunkenness began in some other tavern.
When I get back around to that place,
I'll be completely sober. Meanwhile,
I'm like a bird from another continent, sitting in this aviary.
The day is coming when I fly off,
but who is it now in my ear who hears my voice?
Who says words with my mouth?
Who looks out with my eyes? What is the soul?
I cannot stop asking.
If I could taste one sip of an answer,
I could break out of this prison for drunks.
I didn't come here of my own accord, and I can't leave that way.
Whoever brought me here, will have to take me home.
This poetry. I never know what I'm going to say.
I don't plan it.
When I'm outside the saying of it,
I get very quiet and rarely speak at all.

Whoever Brought Me Here

All day I think about it, then at night I say it.
Where did I come from, and what am I supposed to be doing?
I have no idea.
My soul is from elsewhere, I'm sure of that,
and I intend to end up there.
This drunkenness began in some other tavern.
When I get back around to that place,
I'll be completely sober. Meanwhile,
I'm like a bird from another continent, sitting in this aviary.
The day is coming when I fly off,
but who is it now in my ear who hears my voice?
Who says words with my mouth?
Who looks out with my eyes? What is the soul?
I cannot stop asking.
If I could taste one sip of an answer,
I could break out of this prison for drunks.
I didn't come here of my own accord, and I can't leave that way.
Whoever brought me here, will have to take me home.
This poetry. I never know what I'm going to say.
I don't plan it.
When I'm outside the saying of it,
I get very quiet and rarely speak at all.

With Passion

With
passion pray. With
passion work. With passion make love.
With passion eat and drink and dance and play.
Why look like a dead fish
in this ocean
of God?

You Personify God's Message

You personify God's message.
You reflect the King's face.
There is nothing in the universe that you are not
Everything you want, look for it within yourselfyou
are that.

Your Grief....

Your grief for what youve lost holds a mirror
up to where you're bravely working.
Expecting the worst, you look and instead,
here's the joyful face youve been wanting to see.
Your hand opens and closes and opens and closes.
If it were always a fist or always stretched open,
you would be paralyzed.
Your deepest presence is in every small contracting and expand
the two as beautifully balanced and coordinated
as birdwings.

Your Grief....

Your grief for what youve lost holds a mirror
up to where you're bravely working.
Expecting the worst, you look and instead,
here's the joyful face youve been wanting to see.
Your hand opens and closes and opens and closes.
If it were always a fist or always stretched open,
you would be paralyzed.
Your deepest presence is in every small contracting and expand
the two as beautifully balanced and coordinated
as birdwings.

Zero Circle

Be helpless, dumbfounded,
Unable to say yes or no.
Then a stretcher will come from grace
To gather us up.
We are too dull-eyed to see that beauty
If we say we can, we're lying.
If we say No, we don't see it,
That No will behead us
And shut tight our window onto spirit.
So let us rather not be sure of anything,
Besides ourselves, and only that, so
Miraculous beings come running to help.
Crazed, lying in a zero circle, mute,
We shall be saying finally,
With tremendous eloquence, Lead us.
When we have totally surrendered to that beauty,
We shall be a mighty kindness.